THE PARADOX

OF

GEORGE ORWELL

THE PARADOX

OF

GEORGE ORWELL

by

Richard J. Voorhees

Purdue University Studies

Humanities Series

ACKNOWLEDGMENTS

For permission to quote from books and articles, I make grateful acknowledgment to the following:

The Bodley Head, Ltd. From *Studies in a Dying Culture,* by Christopher Caudwell, copyright, 1947, by John Lane, The Bodley Head. Reprinted by permission of The Bodley Head. Acknowledgment also to Hillary House Publishers, Ltd.

Brandt & Brandt. From *Down and Out in Paris and London,* by George Orwell, published by Harcourt, Brace & Company, copyright, 1933, by George Orwell; from *Burmese Days,* by George Orwell, published by Harcourt, Brace & Company, copyright, 1934, by George Orwell; from *Coming Up for Air,* by George Orwell, copyright, 1950, by Harcourt, Brace & Company; from *Nineteen Eighty-Four,* by George Orwell, copyright, 1949, by Harcourt, Brace & Company. Reprinted by permission of Brandt & Brandt.

William Collins Sons & Company, Ltd. From *The English People,* by George Orwell, copyright, 1947, by William Collins Sons & Company, Ltd. Reprinted by permission of William Collins Sons & Company, Ltd.

Doubleday & Company. From *On a Chinese Screen,* by Somerset Maugham, copyright, 1922, by The George H. Doran Company. Reprinted by permission of Doubleday & Company.

Harcourt, Brace & Company. From *Animal Farm,* by George Orwell, copyright, 1946, by Harcourt, Brace & Company; from *A Clergyman's Daughter,* by George Orwell, published, 1960, by Harcourt Brace & Company; from *Dickens, Dali and Others,* by George Orwell, copyright, 1946, by George Orwell; from *Homage to Catalonia,* by George Orwell, copyright, 1952, by Sonia Brownell

Orwell; from *The Road to Wigan Pier,* by George Orwell, published, 1958, by Harcourt, Brace & Company; from *Shooting an Elephant,* by George Orwell, copyright, 1950, by Sonia Brownell Orwell; from *Such, Such Were the Joys,* by George Orwell, copyright, 1953, by Sonia Brownell Orwell; from *Principles and Persuasions,* by Anthony West, copyright, 1957, by Anthony West. Reprinted by permission of Harcourt, Brace & Company.

The Macmillan Company. From *Darkness at Noon,* by Arthur Koestler, copyright, 1941, by The Macmillan Company. Reprinted by permission of The Macmillan Company.

Methuen and Company, Ltd. From *The Writer and the Absolute,* by Wyndham Lewis, copyright, 1952, by Methuen and Company, Ltd. Reprinted by permission of Methuen and Company, Ltd. Acknowledgment also to Hillary House Publishers, Ltd.

The New Republic. From "Anthony West as Critic," by Donald Malcolm, *The New Republic,* April 15, 1957, copyright by The New Republic, Inc. Reprinted by permission of *The New Republic.*

Partisan Review. From "Decency and Death," by Isaac Rosenfeld, *Partisan Review,* May, 1950, copyright, 1950, by *Partisan Review.* Reprinted by permission of *Partisan Review.*

Secker and Warburg, Ltd. From *The Lion and The Unicorn,* by George Orwell, copyright, 1941, by Secker and Warburg, Ltd. Reprinted by permission of Secker and Warburg, Ltd.

For permission to reprint articles that have appeared in their pages, I wish to thank the following:

The Canadian Forum. For "Orwell and Power-Hunger," *The Canadian Forum,* July, 1956, copyright, 1956, by Canadian Forum, Ltd. Reprinted by permission of *The Canadian Forum.*

The Commonweal. For "Orwell's Secular Crusade," *The Commonweal,* January 28, 1955, copyright by The Commonweal Publishing Company. Reprinted by permission of *The Commonweal.*

Duke University Press. For "George Orwell: Rebellion and Responsibility," *The South Atlantic Quarterly,* October, 1954, copyright, 1954, by Duke University Press. Reprinted by permission of Duke University Press.

The National Council of Teachers of English. For *"Nineteen Eighty-Four:* No Failure of Nerve," College English, November,

1956, copyright, 1956, by The National Council of Teachers of English. Reprinted by permission of The National Council of Teachers of English.

University of Nebraska Press. For "George Orwell as Critic," *Prairie Schooner,* Summer, 1954, copyright, 1954, by University of Nebraska Press. Reprinted by permission of University of Nebraska Press.

Finally, I wish to thank Indiana University, where, in a somewhat different form, the manuscript was submitted as a doctoral thesis, and Professor Robert G. Kelly, Department of English, a most capable and conscientious director.

To S. A. Levin, M. D.

PREFACE

THREE books, as well as dozens of articles, have already been written about George Orwell. All of the books are by British writers who knew him personally. Laurence Brander *(George Orwell,* 1954) and John Atkins *(George Orwell,* 1954) became acquainted with him during the War. Christopher Hollis *(A Study of George Orwell,* 1956) was at Eton with him and also saw him off and on for the rest of his life. Although these books have the advantage of first-hand knowledge, this knowledge is limited by the respect of the authors for Orwell's wish that there be no biography of him; they have included in their books only those facts that have been previously recorded, some of them by Orwell's friends, but most of them by Orwell himself here and there in his published work.

The facts, in brief, are these. George Orwell was born in Bengal in 1903. His father was an official in the Indian Civil Service. Both of his parents were Scottish, and he was christened Eric Hugh Blair. (When he was twenty-seven, he took as a pseudonym the name by which he is generally known, Orwell from a river in Suffolk near which he once lived, and George as a typical English name.) At the age of eight he was sent as a scholarship boy to the preparatory school on the South Coast of England which he described in the essay "Such, Such Were the Joys." At twelve he won scholarships for both Eton and Wellington, and chose to go to Eton. He always said that he did no work at Eton, although he read widely among books of his own choosing, yet he managed to keep a middle place among a form of scholarship boys. Advised by his tutor not to go on to a university, he enlisted in the Indian Imperial Police. He was sent to Burma, where he served from 1922 to 1927. His experiences there furnished the material for his first novel, *Burmese Days.* The Indian Imperial Police had heavy duties, being responsible for detective work and prison administration, as well as general law and order. Orwell took his duties very seriously, but he found himself unsuited for the job of governing a subject people. Moreover, the climate, he considered, was ruining his health. Given leave after the usual five years, he returned to Europe and later resigned.

For a year and a half he lived in Paris, writing (but not publishing) novels and short stories. Afterwards there followed several years of poverty, during which Orwell was dishwasher, private tutor, teacher in cheap schools, clerk in a book store, and tramp. The experiences of these years led to the autobiographical *Down and Out in Paris and London* and to the novels *A Clergyman's Daughter* and *Keep the Aspidistra Flying*. In 1935 he settled in the country and combined writing with other occupations, first running a pub and then keeping a small general store. In 1936 he was commissioned to investigate unemployment in the North of England. *The Road to Wigan Pier* is the result of his investigation. Before the end of the year he went to Spain to observe the Civil War, but he stayed to fight in it on the Republican side. *Homage to Catalonia* records his observations of the fighting in Spain and the operations of totalitarianism. On his return to England he wrote *Coming Up for Air*, a book which looks both backward to the comparative peacefulness of the late nineteenth and early twentieth centuries and forward to World War II.

Though rejected on grounds of health when he volunteered for the British Army, Orwell served in the Home Guard. During the War years he wrote newspaper and magazine articles and talks for the Indian Service of the B.B.C. and, as the European War was coming to a close, *Animal Farm*. In 1947 he went to live on a Scottish island. Two years later the bronchial and lung disorders which had troubled him all his life made it necessary for him to enter a tuberculosis sanitorium in Gloucestershire and then University College Hospital in London. In spite of his illness, he managed to finish *Nineteen Eighty-Four*. As soon as he had sufficient time and strength, he planned to turn from political writing to writing about human relationships in the manner of Conrad. He was to go to Switzerland for further medical treatment, but the day before he was scheduled to leave, he suffered a fatal hemorrhage. In accord with his request, he was buried in an English village churchyard.

Besides chapters which give the above biographical information in greater detail, the three British books have chapters which analyze each of Orwell's works or groups of works in turn. In my own study I have tried to pursue certain lines of paradox which run through Orwell's life and writing. Because Orwell was a paradoxical writer, he has made contradictory and sometimes very queer impressions on readers and critics. Some of them see him as the embodiment of common sense, some as a hero of liberalism, some as a peevish or perverse eccentric. In an effort to help to clarify Orwell and his books, I have explored in three chapters the following paradoxes.

First, Orwell was a rebel with a remarkably strong sense of responsibility. When he was a child, he revolted against the religious teachings and the discipline of his school. The mature equivalents of his boyhood feelings were his hostile attitudes toward organized religion and toward social, political, and cultural authority. As charitable organizations, Orwell thought, the churches were demoralizing; as moral and political forces, they were puritanic and reactionary; as a spiritual force, they were worthless. Orwell felt contempt for the aristocracy and resented every sort of governmental and social pressure. His rebellion extended even to literary criticism: he rejected the usual critical assumptions and denied that criticism was a force, good or bad, in culture. Because Orwell's rebellion was comprehensive and occasionally violent, some critics have considered him to be neurotic. Their theories, however, attribute to him feelings which his whole life and all of his writing contradict. Orwell's sense of responsibility was eminently sane and practical. He lived with the poor to find out exactly what poverty was like. Though deficient in religious feeling himself, he recognized what society loses when religious feeling deteriorates. And despite his rejection of all political orthodoxies, he was closely engaged in the political issues of his time

Second, Orwell was horrified by large concentrations of power, but he was determined to resist them. In the first stage of his career he was preoccupied with the evils of imperialistic power. In the last stage he was preoccupied with the evils of totalitarian power. The preoccupation with totalitarianism, however, was not a surrender: in *Nineteen Eighty-Four* he does not predict universal totalitarianism in our time. To begin with, he was always dubious about the value of political prediction. Besides, in *Nineteen Eighty-Four* he takes countless details from totalitarianism just as it was at the time of the book.

Third, Orwell crusaded for a socialistic society, yet he had important reservations about socialism. The inequalities and inefficiencies of capitalism proved to him the urgent need for socialism. Socialists would have to contend, however, not only with privilege and tradition, but with certain types in their own ranks, such as crackpots and petty despots. Orwell was confident that socialism would, nevertheless, succeed; but he was not pleased with some of its corollaries. He knew that socialism implied increased mechanization, but he had an aversion to modern machinery. Similarly, he knew that a socialistic government would have to invade areas of life which capitalism does not. He felt, in consequence, a nostalgia for nineteenth-century England, where life was simpler and in some ways freer than it would be in the society toward which he worked.

R. J. V.
West Lafayette, Indiana
November 1, 1960

CONTENTS

CHAPTER 1

Rebellion and Responsibility

i. THE REVOLT AGAINST AUTHORITY

GEORGE ORWELL was perhaps the most paradoxical English writer of his time. He was an intellectual, but he continually damned intellectuals. He was a first-rate political writer in spite of his fundamental horror of politics, and a successful pamphleteer in spite of his constant warnings to his readers to beware of his bias. He was witheringly contemptuous of the majority of socialists; nevertheless, he believed that socialism was the only thing that could save England. In his books he deplored the violence of the modern world, and yet he was nearly killed fighting in the Spanish Civil War. Although in chronically poor health, he performed extraordinary physical labors; although sensitive and discriminating, he endured the vilest kind of surroundings without complaint. The barest facts of his life reveal startling incongruities and sharp contrasts. He graduated from Eton but later worked as a dishwasher. After serving in the Indian Imperial Police in Burma, he lived for some time as a tramp. For thirteen years he wrote novels and essays that did not sell well enough to be reprinted, and then, in the space of three years, he published two best sellers. When at last he had become rich and famous, he retired to a Scottish island.

Of all the paradoxes in Orwell's character, none strikes the reader more strongly than the combination of rebellion and responsibility. Orwell's rebellion started, in a confused and abortive way, when he was a schoolboy. In the posthumous essay "Such, Such Were the Joys" he describes the form and pressure of the school world, and his resistance to it:

> It was not only money that mattered: there were also strength, beauty, charm, athleticism and something called "guts" or "char-

acter," which in reality meant the power to impose your will on others. . . . That was the pattern of school life—a continuous triumph of the strong over the weak. Virtue consisted in winning; it consisted in being bigger, stronger, handsomer, richer, more popular, more elegant, more unscrupulous than other people—in dominating them, bullying them, making them suffer pain, making them look foolish, getting the better of them in every way. Life was hierarchical and whatever happened was right. There were the strong, who deserved to win and always did win, and there were the weak, who deserved to lose and always did lose, everlastingly.

I did not question the prevailing standards, because so far as I could see there were no others. How could the rich, the strong, the elegant, the fashionable, the powerful, be in the wrong? It was their world, and the rules they made for it must be the right ones. And yet from a very early age I was aware of the impossibility of any *subjective* conformity. Always at the center of my heart the inner self seemed to be awake, pointing out the difference between the moral obligation and the psychological *fact*. It was the same in all matters, worldly or other-worldly. Take religion, for instance. You were supposed to love God, and I did not question this. . . . But I was well aware that I did not love Him. On the contrary, I hated Him. . . .[1]

In time the childish hatreds were moderated, and Orwell became about as cool-headed as it is possible for a controversialist to be. Still, an antagonism toward religion and toward authority, social, political, and cultural, was one of the fundamental feelings of his whole adult life.

Running through Orwell's writing like a pattern are criticisms of the churches in three of their capacities: as charitable, as moral and political, and as spiritual institutions.

His experiences as a tramp convinced him that the charity of the churches takes away more than it gives. He realized, however, that this is not altogether the fault of the churches, that there is (at least in the modern world) something disagreeable about receiving charity, and that those who receive it are therefore less likely to be grateful than resentful. Describing a scene in one of the missions where the tramps are given tea, Orwell says, "I am sure . . . that it was given in good spirit, without any intention of humiliating us; so in fairness we ought to have been grateful—still, we were not."[2] More often, however, the spirit in which the charity was given was dubious, at least to Orwell. "It is curious," he says apropos of a group of people who come into a flophouse without invitation and hold a service, "how people take it for granted that they have a right to preach at you and pray over you as soon as your income falls below a certain level."[3]

Orwell believed that tramps, patronized by missionaries who tell them that Christ has a soft spot in His heart even for rough men like them, actually hate their benefactors bitterly. There is a scene in *Down and Out in Paris and London* where the tramps whom Orwell has joined break up the religious ceremonies that follow the tea that they are given in church.

> . . . the service began. And instantly, as though at a signal, the tramps began to behave in the most outrageous manner. . . . All round the gallery men lolled in their pews, laughed, chattered, leaned over and flicked pellets of bread among the congregation. . . .[4]

The scene is a rather dreadful one, but Orwell sees the tramps' side of it: they have been humiliated by the tea, and they are taking their revenge. There was only one clergyman whom Orwell's tramp friends admired.

> He was shy and embarrassed, and did not speak except for a brief good evening; he simply hurried down the line of men, thrusting a meal ticket upon each, and not waiting to be thanked. The consequence was that, for once, there was genuine gratitude. . . . Someone . . . called out: "Well, *he'll* never be a —— bishop!" — this intended, of course, as a warm compliment.[5]

Even when they were being paid for their goods and services, Orwell thought, religious or quasi-religious bodies acted as though they were giving charity. The Salvation Army hostels, he says, charged as much for a bed as any common lodging-house did, but they made the tramps pay extra in regimentation: they were waked and sent to bed by whistles and herded so close together in the dormitories that they could scarcely get a decent night's sleep. The result was that the men who went to them became hopeless if they were not so already. As for the YMCA, Orwell's way of describing an unpleasant charitable organization is to say that it has a "nasty YMCA atmosphere."[6] In *A Clergyman's Daughter* he indicates the desperation of the heroine's loneliness by saying that there were even times when she considered joining the YWCA.

As political institutions, the churches, Orwell thought, did much more harm than they did as charitable ones. He knew, of course, that there was a Christian socialism which is dedicated not to the charity which he deplored, but to making that charity unnecessary. Nonetheless, he considered that the main powers of the churches were in an instinctive alliance with everything that was reactionary and even Fascistic.

> Behind all the ballyhoo that is talked about . . . the "materialism" of the working classes lies the simple intention of those with money or privilege to cling to them. . . . The pious ones, from the Pope to the yogis of California, are great on the "change of heart," much more reassuring from their point of view than a change in the economic system.[7]

The moral force of the churches was, Orwell thought, as hostile to the working man as the political force, since the morality of the churches was puritanic, and the working classes are anything but puritans. They have a passion for gambling, they drink as much as they can afford, they love bawdy jokes, and (Orwell states it with a kind of pride) they use the foulest language in the world. That half of the activities they enjoy are constricted by absurd regulations like the lottery acts and the licensing laws is due, Orwell thought, to the influence of the churches on English life. The temper of this influence seems summed up for Orwell by the old churchwarden who came rushing out of St. Martin's in the Fields to rage at the pavement artist who had copied Botticelli's Venus on the sidewalk: "Do you think that we can have that obscenity outside God's holy house?"[8]

The negative force of puritanism was, Orwell thought, the only spiritual force which the churches of England were capable of generating. He attributed their spiritual negation, not to a scepticism among the mass of English people for which science is responsible, but to a sheer indifference for which the churches themselves are responsible. During the Industrial Revolution, he says, the Anglican Church began to lose touch with the mass of its members. Two or three generations later it was practically a "preserve of the landed gentry."[9] In recent times, Orwell believed, the Nonconformist sects have also lost influence.

Supposing the average clergyman to be what Orwell makes him out to be, the churches would be hard put indeed to exert any spiritual influence on the average man. In Orwell's essays the Anglican clergyman is a selfish fellow whose interests in what is established go beyond the Church. The dissenting clergyman is a fool ("Like most Nonconformist missionaries, he was a complete ass but quite a good fellow").[10] In Orwell's novel *A Clergyman's Daughter* the Anglican rector is both selfish and foolish. At Millborough the Reverend Edward Hare has one of the poorest livings in the whole Church. Nevertheless, he is an archreactionary. The whole modern world disgusts him, so much so that half of the time he does not live in it.

> When her father began to talk about . . . things that had happened "when I was up at Oxford," there was nothing more to be done with him. It meant that he had slipped into an imaginary golden past in which . . . he seemed to forget that he was only a poverty-stricken country Rector—that he was not a young man of family with estates and reversions at his back.[11]

The Rector's household is a shabby-genteel one in which the silver dish-covers are heirlooms and most of the knives, forks, and spoons come from Woolworth's. The head of such a household obviously has no business speculating, but the Rector does so, with such an unerring sense of the wrong stocks that each year he loses enough money to pay a curate's salary. This disturbs him no end (though he is always confident of the next investment). Running up bills with tradesmen, however, does not bother him a bit. When Dorothy tells him that the butcher is getting importunate, he says,

> It is simply abominable how these people take it upon themselves to behave nowadays—abominable! But there you are. . . . That is the kind of thing that we are exposed to in this delightful century. That is democracy—progress, they are pleased to call it. . . . Tell him at once that you are taking your account elsewhere. That is the only way to treat these people.[12]

Though reactionary in most respects, the rector is out of sympathy with the traditions to which his parishioners cling.

> The Rector had . . . a perfect abhorrence of Harvest Festivals. He had even lost a valuable parishioner—a Mr. Toagis, a . . . retired market gardener—through his dislike, as he said, of seeing

his church dressed up to imitate a coster's stall. . . . The
previous summer Mr. Toagis had succeeded in growing a perfect
leviathan of a pumpkin . . .   so enormous that it took two
men to lift it. This monstrous object dwarfed the altar and took
all the color out of the East window. . . . Mr. Toagis hung
about the church at all hours, unable to tear himself away . . .
even bringing friends to admire it. . . . But when the Rector
saw the pumpkin he was seriously angry, and ordered "that revolting
thing" to be removed at once. Mr. Toagis had instantly "gone
chapel," and he and his heirs were lost to the church forever.[13]

There are no ties between Mr. Hare and his congregation at any
level of class or feeling. He despises the working class. (" 'This is
a valid sacrament,' he seemed to be saying, 'and it is my duty to
administer it to you. But remember that I am only your priest, not
your friend.' ")[14] He is envious of the upper classes. All in all, Mr.
Hare has managed in his twenty-three years as Rector to reduce his
congregation from six hundred to two hundred.

Even among the remaining two hundred, religion has deterio-
rated sadly. As she goes about her duties in her father's parish,
Dorothy Hare finds people who make great professions of piety,
but some of them do so in the hopes of getting a little money from
the poor box and others for the sake of gossiping with Dorothy
when she makes her rounds. A few of them are quite honest in their
professions of faith, but their piety is bound up with the idea of
poor boxes and gossip in the sky. The heaven of the most devout
working-class wife in the parish is material in the most explicit
detail, having not only pearly gates and golden streets, but also
such luxuries as silk clothes, rich foods, and silver dishes that do
not have to be washed. Where it is not mere pretense, religion is a
pitiful travesty.

Just as religion had declined in Mr. Hare's parish, it had declined, Orwell thought, all over England. Two out of three Englishmen, although they have retained the gentleness and decency of
the Christian tradition, although they regard some of the ethical
admonitions of Christ as axiomatic, although they may have even
kept a vague theism and a fuzzy belief in an after-life, have lost
contact with Christianity as a religion. Brought up against it by
accident, they are likely to be embarrassed or annoyed. (When
Orwell wishes to indicate how uncomfortable the average Englishman now feels in the presence of poetry, he says that the very name

of poetry "creates in advance the same sort of bad impression as the word 'God' or a parson's dog-collar.")[15] Talking of one of the tramps whom he met in a mission, he remarks that he "could pronounce the words 'the dear Lord Jesus' with less shame than anyone I ever saw."[16] (Even this man saves his face by passing out hymn books as though he were dealing playing cards.)

Orwell's obvious exaggeration of the extent to which English society has been secularized is in one way probably a wish-fulfillment. Since the churches were reactionary organizations, the faster they lost their adherents (he would feel), the better. At the same time it is probable that he honestly underestimated the number of adherents that the churches had to lose. Because religious convictions were impossible for Orwell himself, he thought that they were possible for very few other people. He could therefore fail to see strong religious feelings even when he met them head-on. Could he have been made aware of his failure to perceive religious feelings, he would have minded it only because of the social implications of the feelings.

In the religious feelings themselves he had almost no interest, not even the detached and ironical sympathy with religious doctrine and ritual such as an Anatole France or a Santayana had. This lack of interest is evident in *Burmese Days*. Like E. M. Forster in *A Passage to India*, Orwell in *Burmese Days* tries to make an Oriental country intelligible to a Western reader. Unlike Forster, he does almost nothing with the religious area of the country's culture. One would not expect a close equivalent of the marvelous scenes of the religious ceremonies in *A Passage to India*, but there is not even a remote equivalent of them in *Burmese Days*. The few satirical passages on religion in the book are probably the result of his maddening personal experiences with Buddhist priests (at the time they were the professional British-baiters among the Burmese); the general disregard of the whole religious area of the Burmese mind is probably due to the turn of his own mind.

Like his boyish rebellion against God, the patriarchs, and the prophets, Orwell's rebellion against the "well-born," the rich, and the supposedly wise in the school world had its mature equivalent. First of all, there was his quarrel with the British aristocracy. In the midst of his fight with the new totalitarianism that threatened freedom from the outside he found time to attack the old aristocracy that, he thought, threatened it from the inside. Sometimes his hostility to the British aristocrat seems greater than his hostility to the Russian Communist, because he did not expect anything good from the Communist, whereas he considered that he had a right to expect something from the aristocrat. It was not merely their ordinary selfishness, but their loss of seriousness, that caused him to feel such scorn for British aristocrats generally. His analysis of the Spanish Civil War is, for the most part, as calm as it is keen; he soon saw what the Communists were up to, but his exposure of them is fairly dispassionate. When, however, he learns that an English duchess, staying at expensive hotels, has failed to find anything very abnormal about life in wartime Madrid or Barcelona, aside from a shortage of butter, he cannot resist an expression of his contempt: "I hope they found some butter for the Duchess."[17]

It was partly because he regarded the constable as the representative of the ruling classes that Orwell took a jaundiced view of the English police (as a law-enforcing body, the English police were, he thought, remarkably humane compared with their counterparts in other countries). He had, he said, no particular love for the "worker" of Communist literature, "but when I see an actual flesh-and-blood worker in conflict with his natural enemy, the policeman, I do not have to ask myself which side I am on."[18]

Orwell's mature rebellion also expressed itself in a resentment of any sort of governmental or social pressure. As the policeman is the enemy of the worker, the government official is the enemy of the intellectual, interfering with him whenever it is possible to do so and always suspicious of him. English officialdom, Orwell thought, would have liked to keep intellectuals out of important positions in World War II and finally let them in only when it was clear that they were necessary to the war effort. Even in his last essays he calls the government "our rulers," as if England were a country run by a monarch and his court. There is, in fact, an anarchistic strain in Orwell which comes out even in so light a piece as his review of a new edition of Edward Lear, where he quotes Aldous Huxley's remark that the "they" of the limericks represents conformity, public opinion, etc., and then adds that smashing the old man from Whitehaven who danced a quadrille with a raven is exactly the kind of thing that "they" would do. The anarchism takes a comic and fantastic form in *Coming Up for Air,* when the hero, running away from his wife and the modern world for a week, feels himself pursued not only by Stalin and Hitler, but also by the Bank of England and various officials of the British government.

The rebellion appears even in *Animal Farm*. Although an attack on totalitarianism, *Animal Farm* is a long way from being a defense of capitalism, British or otherwise. Of course, Orwell is shooting mainly at the Russian Revolution and its results, but he also fires some shots at reactions in other countries to the events in Russia. When the animals first get control of the farm, the people of the countryside predict that they will not be able to run it and will therefore starve. Then, when it is clear that the beasts are not starving, the people circulate rumors about the terrible wickedness of the new establishment: the animals torture one another with red-hot horseshoes, have their females in common, and practice cannibalism. When the anthem of Animal Farm, "The Beasts of England," becomes popular on other farms as well, the human beings are infuriated and frightened, but they pretend to think that the song is altogether absurd. They cannot understand, they say, "how even animals could bring themselves to sing such contemptible rubbish."[19] In the last few pages of the book Orwell attacks the capitalist from another angle. The pigs, after replacing the tyranny of Farmer Jones with their own, give a dinner for some neighboring farmers, one of whom explains in a two-page speech that they can get along in jolly fashion because they have, after all, the same objectives. He winds up his speech with a joke which sets the table aroar: "If you have your lower animals to contend with, we have our lower classes."[20] The early history of Animal Farm, then, is partly a satire of the Tory protesting against any form of social change because he fears and hates it; the later history is partly a satire of the Tory wanting to get along well with dictatorships because it is good business to do so.

Orwell carried his rebellion against authority even into his literary criticism. The questions with which conventional criticism occupies itself—questions of the stature of a writer or the structure of a work, for instance—seemed to Orwell to be frivolous, or uninteresting, or unanswerable. Critical authorities were running a racket (Orwell would have said "swindle") rather like those of social, political, and religious authorities. What they had to say about literature was, in Orwell's eyes, likely to be silly, like the remarks of the English duchess in Madrid, or beside the point and, in any case, beyond proof, like the speculations of the theologians on the nature of God.

Orwell's essay on "Lear, Tolstoy and the Fool" illustrates his attitude toward the question of literary greatness. The first four pages of this long essay are devoted to a summary of Tolstoy's attack on Shakespeare's work as a whole and on *King Lear* in particular. In *Shakespeare and the Drama* Tolstoy says that *Lear* is stupid, verbose, vulgar, full of silly jokes and incredible episodes. Shakespeare picked up a few dramatic tricks during his acting days, but he never learned to create character or to make language and action arise naturally out of situations. His construction is untidy, his morals are debased, and his emotions are insincere. Hence he does not even approach Tolstoy's requirements for the ordinary respectable artist, much less those for the genius that Shakespeare is generally considered to be. To show how Tolstoy operates, Orwell quotes a specimen paragraph:

> Lear walks about the heath and says words which are meant to express his despair: he desires that the winds should blow so hard that they (the winds) should crack their cheeks and that the rain should flood everything, that lightning should singe his white head, and that the thunder flatten the world and destroy all germs "that make ungrateful man"! The fool keeps uttering still more senseless words. Enter Kent: Lear says that for some reason during this storm all criminals shall be found out and convicted. Kent, still unrecognized by Lear, endeavors to persuade him to take refuge in a hovel. At this point the fool utters a prophecy in no wise related to the situation and they all depart.[21]

Tolstoy's last word on *Lear* is that if anybody not hypnotized by Shakespeare's reputation were to read the play to the end, the only emotions he would feel would be "aversion and weariness." And the same would be true of "all the other extolled dramas of Shakespeare, not to mention the senseless dramatized tales, *Pericles, Twelfth Night, The Tempest, Cymbeline, Troilus and Cressida.*"[22]

One's first reaction to all this, Orwell remarks naturally enough, is that Tolstoy is saying "something demonstrably untrue."[23] But he denies that this first feeling is correct. "In reality there is no kind of evidence or argument by which one can show that Shakespeare, or any other writer, is 'good.' Nor is there any way of definitely proving that—for instance—Warwick Deeping is 'bad.' "[24] All efforts to show that one writer is better than another are, therefore, a waste of time. In his long essay on Dickens, Orwell is interested in discussing some of the differences between Tolstoy and Dickens, but not in giving one of the novelists a high and the other a low mark.

> You cannot hold an imaginary conversation with a Dickens character as you can with, say Pierre Bezoukhov. And this is not merely because of Tolstoy's greater seriousness, for there are also comic characters that you can imagine yourself talking to—Bloom for instance. . . . It is because Dickens's characters have no mental life. . . . They never learn, never speculate. Perhaps the most meditative of his characters is Paul Dombey, and his thoughts are mush. Does that mean that Tolstoy's novels are "better" than Dickens's? The truth is that it is absurd to make such comparisons in terms of "better" and "worse." If I were forced to compare Tolstoy with Dickens, I should say that Tolstoy's appeal will probably be wider in the long run, because Dickens is scarcely intelligible outside the English-speaking culture; on the other hand, Dickens is able to reach simple people, which Tolstoy is not. Tolstoy's characters can cross a frontier. Dickens's can be portrayed on a cigarette-card. But one is no more obliged to choose between them than between a sausage and a rose.[25]

The only thing that can be said for certain about the whole question of literary "greatness," Orwell concludes, is that some books endure and others do not. Of course, it is possible to speculate that one writer will outlast another or be more widely read, as Orwell speculates that Tolstoy will in the long run be more widely read than Dickens. But Orwell does not make his bets on any literary basis, even when he puts his money on the same men that orthodox critics put theirs on. And he often flouts the critical odds. Somerset Maugham, he considers, will last as long as James Joyce, T. S. Eliot, or D. H. Lawrence; *Uncle Tom's Cabin* will outlast anything of Virginia Woolf or George Moore.

It follows that the usual questions about literary structure are just about as pointless as those about literary stature. It is possible, Orwell said in effect, to show that a work has a good or bad structure. But since the strength of a work does not depend upon any sort of literary value, but on "some indefinable quality, a sort of literary vitamin," why bother to demonstrate that the structure of a work is good or bad? If Dickens is "never better than when he is building up some character who will later on be forced to act inconsistently,"[26] then the parts of Dickens are simply greater than the whole, and that is that. In the same way, "It is futile to object that the superfluous detail in Dickens is rococo—one might as well make the same objection to a wedding cake. Either you like it or you do not like it."[27] That, as far as Orwell is concerned, sums up all esthetic preference.

Criticism which, consciously or unconsciously, uses esthetic judgments merely as a mask for other kinds of judgments interests Orwell more than criticism which is honestly esthetic. Tolstoy's criticism of Shakespeare is, he thinks, an example of such criticism —and a very valuable one for what it tells the reader, not about the playwright Shakespeare, but about the man Tolstoy. If, however, criticism is the expression of preferences which are either inexplicable or hypocritical, one is bound to suspect sometimes, Orwell says, that the whole of literary criticism is one huge fraud. Whether or not the critic is talking through his hat, he is ultimately talking to himself: in his rebellion against the assumptions of conventional literary criticism Orwell rejects the assumption that criticism exerts a force on literature. "Lear, Tolstoy and the Fool" has the following coda:

> But finally the most striking thing is how little difference it all makes. As I said earlier, one cannot *answer* Tolstoy's pamphlet, at least not on its main counts. There is no argument by which one can defend a poem. It defends itself by surviving, or it is indefensible. And if this test is valid, I think the verdict in Shakespeare's case must be "not guilty." Like every other writer, Shakespeare will be forgotten sooner or later, but it is unlikely that a heavier indictment will ever be brought against him. Tolstoy was perhaps the most admired literary man of his age, and he was certainly not its least able pamphleteer. He turned all his powers of denunciation against Shakespeare, like the guns of a battleship firing simultaneously. And with what result? Forty years later Shakespeare is still there, completely unaffected, and of the attempt to demolish him nothing remains except the yellowing pages of a pamphlet which hardly anyone has read, and which would be forgotten altogether if Tolstoy had not also been the author of *War and Peace* and *Anna Karenina*.[28]

ii. THE QUESTION OF NEUROSIS

Including as it did cultural and religious authorities as well as social and political ones, Orwell's rebellion was obviously thorough. Some commentators on Orwell consider that it was excessive. Anthony West considers that it was neurotic. According to West, Orwell suffered during his stay at the school which he calls "Crossgates" in "Such, Such Were the Joys" a psychic wound which continued to ache all his life long. In this sixty-page autobiographical essay Orwell certainly makes clear that his years at Crossgates were, on the whole, unhappy ones. He was physically uncomfortable much of the time; he was bullied; he was humiliated by the snobbery of boys who had more money than he had. Taking his cue from the last point, West comments: ". . . the hurt child's feeling that money is the measure of all things . . . is treated as the final truth about the adult world in both *Down and Out in Paris and London* and *Keep the Aspidistra Flying*."[29] *Keep the Aspidistra Flying* is, West says, the story of Gordon Comstock's attempting to beat the money system by degrading himself, finding that degradation does not work, and then beating the system by conforming cynically.

> But Orwell writes this "happy" ending without much conviction; his mind is already warming to the idea of a universal smashup. It would destroy the middle class, which had invented the horrible educational machine that had hurt him, and it would destroy the whole world of money values, in which he felt himself inadequate.[30]

(By the time of *Coming Up for Air*, which was published in 1939, Orwell's mind must have been red-hot.) Of course, the British withstood the War—the Blitz, the short rations, and all the rest of it—and although English civilization was altered by the War, it was not destroyed. "It would be unfair, perhaps, to say that Orwell was disappointed," West writes, "but at any rate he felt cheated."[31] In a review of West's book, Donald Malcolm came to the defense of Orwell and other writers whom West had attacked. Having noted the fact that throughout the essay West's knowledge of Orwell's unconscious mind is much better than Orwell's own, Malcolm remarks:

> Orwell's conscious mind wrote the following during the bombings in 1941: "In whatever shape England emerges from the war, it will be deeply tinged with the characteristics that I have spoken of earlier. The intellectuals who hope to see it Russianized or Germanized will be disappointed. The gentleness, the hypocrisy, the

> thoughtlessness, the reverence for law and the hatred of uniforms will remain, along with the suet puddings and the misty skies."[32]

But this kind of evidence does not bother West a bit. One of the principles of his criticism, he says, is the following:

> The falsifications he [the writer] indulges in while fabricating the persona he presents for public consumption generally show up in his books as falsities, and if one is aware of the deliberate or compulsive distortions that shape his life, one is the better equipped to judge by how much his work is a contribution to knowledge and by how much it is a simple reflection of his psychological necessities.[33]

Since West's use of this principle enables him to demolish Dickens (in the last half dozen lines of the Dickens essay he decides, after all, not to, and says that Dickens, with all his faults, was still a genius), it is no surprise that he can easily chop Orwell into small bits. But, really, the size of the writer is not relevant. The special advantage of West's method, as Malcolm says, is that it makes it so simple for the critic to prove that the writer is suffering from compulsive distortions. "Having proved to his own satisfaction that Orwell was deranged . . . Mr. West feels free to examine *Nineteen Eighty-Four* exclusively in terms of Orwell's 'psychological necessities.'"[34] The result of the examination is that Big Brother, the dictator of *Nineteen Eighty-Four,* turns out to be simply Bingo, the hated and feared wife of the headmaster as Crossgates; Room 101 in the Ministry of Love, the headmaster's study; and just about everything else in *Nineteen Eighty-Four,* something else in "Such, Such Were the Joys." And the reason? "Whether he knew it or not, what he did in *Nineteen Eighty-Four* was to send everybody in England to an enormous Crossgates to be as miserable as he had been."[35]

West manages to make out a case against Orwell only by applying a remarkable ingenuity to the novels and ignoring much in the essays. At the beginning of his own essay, which begins as a review of *Keep the Aspidistra Flying,* he says that the novel was published in England in 1936,

> the year he [Orwell] said in his essay "Why I Write" was the critical one in his career, because he felt that during it he discovered what he had to do. This was to write political books designed "to push the world in a certain direction," to alter people's idea of the society that they should strive after.[36]

But given, of course, West's principle that Orwell did not know what he was doing, it is easy to persuade the unwary that Orwell's striving for a better society was really a desire that society be destroyed.

Crossgates was not Oceania; but neither was it Utopia. The headmaster's notion of education was to stuff his scholarship students with scraps of historical information which he knew from past experience would be called for on the examinations for Wellington and Eton. His idea of propriety was to allow the richer boys special favors like birthday cakes and to call the attention of the poorer boys to their financial inferiority. Bingo, the headmaster's wife, was if anything worse than the headmaster himself. Yet most of the boys, while hating Bingo, fawned upon her. "Whenever one had the chance to suck up, one did suck up, and at the first smile one's hatred turned into a sort of cringing love."[37]

The child tends to believe what his elders tell him, and since Bingo and Sim were the most important adults in his world at the time, the boy Orwell readily accepted whatever criticism they made of him.

> All through my boyhood I had a profound conviction that I was no good, that I was wasting my time, wrecking my talents, behaving with monstrous folly and wickedness and ingratitude—and all this was inescapable because I lived among laws which were absolute, like the laws of gravity, but which it was not possible for me to keep.[38]

Orwell was apparently beaten the first time for wetting his bed. (Bedwetting is not unusual for boys of eight, suddenly taken from their homes to a strange place.) He was beaten the second time for boasting that the first had not hurt. The second did not hurt, either, but he wept after it because it "brought home to me, for the first time, the harshness of the environment into which I had been flung. Life was more terrible and I was more wicked than I had ever imagined."[39]

The atmosphere at Crossgates was not only Calvinistic, but Kafkaesque. Some of the rules were not only impossible to keep, but impossible to find out as well. After a commotion about what was evidently group masturbation, with which Orwell had been wrongly connected, one of the masters turned to him and said that he had always seemed to be one of the best boys, and that now he had proved to be a terrible disappointment by turning out to be one of the worst. The boy had no idea of what the master was talking about. "Till then," says Orwell, "I had hoped that I was innocent, and the conviction of sin which now took possession of me was perhaps all the stronger because I did not know what I had done."[40]

But Orwell is not unaware of the risks of exaggeration and self-pity that anyone faces in writing about his childhood. He did not claim that Crossgates was a Dotheboys Hall. Still, he remembered it as a disgusting place. "The overcrowded, underfed, underwashed life that we led *was* disgusting. . . ."[41] Yet in a world which might have shattered him, the boy succeeded in keeping a core of personality intact. The rules of the school world might be the right ones. "And yet . . . I was aware of the impossibility of any *subjective* conformity."[42] His instinct to survive was stronger than his sense of guilt. "I could not invert the existing scale of values, but I could accept my failure and make the best of it."[43] Indeed, he sometimes did better than that. Once, in his refusal to conform even objectively, he struck back at a bully and had no trouble from him thereafter.

The fact is that, although Orwell provided in "Such, Such Were the Joys" sufficient material for the complex-mongers, his days at Crossgates were not all bedwetting and beatings. The title of the essay is ironical, but it is not altogether so. Orwell, as he says, was not a martyr; he did not take pleasure in being hurt. As he later enjoyed things that normal men do—eating, drinking, fishing, smoking—he enjoyed at school whatever natural pleasures he had a chance to.

> The mysterious, terrible dangers were still there. Any morning the black rings [a certain sign of depravity, the boys were told] might appear round your eyes. . . . Only it no longer seemed to matter much. These contradictions can easily exist in the mind of a child, because of its own vitality. It accepts—how could it do otherwise?—the nonsense that its elders tell it, but its youthful body, and the sweetness of the physical world tell it another story.[44]

Some of the masters were decent fellows, and Orwell had pleasant memories of the hours that he spent with them in school and out. He recalled the cricket and the swimming, the expeditions across the Downs to study nature, the exciting railway journeys, the huge teas in country pubs. From the beginning he seemed to have a capacity for happiness, not a hysterical kind as a reaction from intolerable depression, but a quiet and solid kind which he derived from simple things.

The railway journey which took him away from Crossgates for the last time would have been a good one if everything had gone wrong. But everything went right, and the reader should notice not only Orwell's pleasure in his escape, but in all of the small details of it. "Even the detail that my journey-money had been slightly miscalculated, leaving about a shilling over—enough for an unforeseen cup of coffee and a cake or two somewhere on the way—was enough to fill me with bliss."[45] The word *bliss* is, in fact, one of Orwell's favorite words, the one he also uses to describe his state when reading certain books in boyhood or when fishing, and it should be balanced against another one of his favorite words, *swindle*. In boyhood, as in manhood, Orwell had two sides, like anyone else. No man whose childhood was pure misery would have written the following: "I am not able, and I do not want, completely to abandon the world-view that I acquired in childhood. So long as I remain alive I shall continue to . . . love the surface of the earth, and to take a pleasure in solid objects. . . ."[46]

The reader ought also to remember other accounts of English schools in novels and reminiscences by writers like Maugham, Huxley, and Greene. To Greene the world of school was a hellish one; indeed, it was a proof that there really was a hell, so that he believed in hell before he believed in heaven. Even the indomitable Mr. Churchill wrote that his school days were a grey area on the chart of his journey. If every novelist who has complained at some length of being unhappy at school is a neurotic, then so robust a writer as Trollope is, "whether he knew it or not," another neurotic. It is not the indignation that Orwell displays towards some aspects of Crossgates that is remarkable, but the detachment that he exhibits towards others. "I had defective bronchial tubes," he says, "and a lesion in one lung which was not discovered until many years later."[47] A writer suffering from self-pity would have written (and probably would have been nearer the truth) that the lesion was aggravated, if not produced, by the criminally stupid procedure of having a boy with a persistent cough run to cure it, and that the tuberculosis which eventually killed him was caused by the malnutrition and the cold of the school. All his life long Orwell was in more or less poor health. But this did not prevent him, he said, from doing almost anything that he wanted to do. What he wanted to do included some rather difficult things, and his mental constitution compensated for his physical one.

"Such, Such Were the Joys" is, of course, a biographical essay, but it is something more. It is, so to speak, the beginning chapters of Orwell's *David Copperfield*. Besides being a recollection of his own experiences in a certain environment, it is a protest on behalf of others against that environment. Orwell hated tyranny, injustice, and cruelty, and he found all of these at Crossgates. There is, after all, a connection between "Such, Such Were the Joys" and *Nineteen Eighty-Four*, although it is nothing like the one that West seeks to make. *Nineteen Eighty-Four* is an attack on large-scale tyranny, and "Such, Such Were the Joys" is an attack on small-scale tyranny. Ultimately the latter is a report to the end that the children of the future may have a better time than those of Orwell's generation had at school. Conditions have improved since his day in so far as specific abuses have been corrected. But this is not nearly enough. "The real question is whether it is still normal for a school child to live for years amid irrational terrors and lunatic misunderstandings."[48] What West sees as a neurosis is in part the result of Orwell's sense of responsibility.

Until psychoanalysts with diplomas begin to study Orwell, those without diplomas may well go carefully. For the danger of amateur psychoanalysis, as Kenneth Burke said a long time ago, is the temptation to turn it into a game of "heads I win, tails you lose." If the subject exhibits some of the symptoms of the neurotic pattern which is being tailored to fit him, these are set down as evidence. But the symptoms he does not exhibit are also sometimes set down, with the explanation that by not exhibiting them the subject is "compensating." This game is particularly well adapted to the childhood of a writer. If he looks back at it with nostalgia, he can be accused of refusing to grow up (Mark Twain is the classical example, and Evelyn Waugh is a more recent one). If he looks back at it with loathing, he can be accused of such neurosis as West attempts to fasten on Orwell. The tyrant is a neurotic, but so is the hater of tyranny, and everyone, indeed, is a little queer but me and thee.

Isaac Rosenfeld does not detect the excessive response of the neurotic in Orwell's early years, but he detects it with a vengeance in Orwell's later years. Rosenfeld bases his case on his reading of *Nineteen Eighty-Four*. This ingenious reading identifies Orwell with his hero, Winston Smith, and Winston wth Ippolit in Dostoevsky's *The Idiot*. Both characters, says Rosenfeld, defy an intolerable world by yielding to it even more than it demands. And Orwell's retirement to the island in Scotland not only led to his death, but was designed to do so. In effect, he committed suicide in protest against the horrors of contemporary history. Now Rosenfeld's theory of suicide requires a very peculiar reading of *Nineteen Eighty-Four*. The whole point of the scenes between Winston and O'Brien is that Winston does precisely what O'Brien wishes him to, no more and no less. As he tortures Winston, O'Brien explains why he is doing it: it is the only way of making sure that Winston is obeying O'Brien's will and not acting in accord with his own, which may sometimes coincide with O'Brien's. And the identification of Orwell himself with Winston implies, Rosenfeld says, a surrender or repudiation of everything that Orwell had believed in up to *Nineteen Eighty-Four:* "This is Orwell finally yielding up the life-long image, the character and style and habits of reason and restraint. I cannot conceive of a greater despair."[49] I, on the contrary, cannot conceive of Orwell suddenly and completely yielding up the essence of his character in the last year of his life The suicide would have been too ostentatious and melodramatic for a man of Orwell's modesty and common sense, too pointless for a man of his practicality, and too cowardly for a man of his courage.

The curious thing about Rosenfeld's theory is that, while it does not fit Orwell himself or Winston Smith, it perfectly fits Gordon Comstock, the hero of *Keep the Aspidistra Flying*. Because society has given him less than he would have liked, Gordon decides to throw away what he has been given. He refuses a good job in an advertising agency to work in a cheap book store, and life in a decent apartment with his girl Rosemary for life alone in a cold and dirty room. As Wyndham Lewis says, Gordon tries to destroy himself as an economic unit. But then Lewis takes a great leap and, like Rosenfeld, identifies the author of the book with the hero. "Like . . . Gordon Comstock, he preferred the gutter. Gordon Comstock smiling to himself on the bed is the figure, I think, to remember. It is the middle class theatrically, sulkily abasing itself."[50] The truth is that, however well or ill he may represent the middle class,

Gordon does not represent Orwell at all. The point that Orwell is making in *Keep the Aspidistra Flying* is that Gordon is, until the very end of the book, a fool. Far from identifying himself with his hero, he satirizes him: he is a callow and unrealistic prig. It is only in the last chapter of the book that he recognizes the truth of one of Orwell's favorite sayings: half a loaf is better than no bread. One should not exile himself from society or renounce his humanity simply because the circumstances of the moment press hard upon it. In *The Road to Wigan Pier* Orwell has the greatest disgust for people who argued that unemployed workers on the dole should not have children. Why, he demanded, should they cease to be human beings just because they happened to be out of work at the time? *Keep the Aspidistra Flying* is a lesson in how much a man loses by trying to get some of his own back by giving some of himself up. Not that Gordon's renunciation is complete. He wants to renounce money and the money society, but he does not want to renounce Rosemary. He wants a mistress, but he does not want to work for her. And he lacks common sense as much as he lacks responsibility. When he is about to make love to Rosemary and she, suddenly realizing that he has no contraceptive, refuses, he becomes indignant. Under the circumstances, contraception is the only sensible thing, but Gordon wishes to raise a rumpus about money even here. Later, however, Rosemary does give herself to Gordon. When he learns that she is pregnant, he wakes up to the facts of the real world and quits spinning fictions for himself. He marries Rosemary and takes the job with the advertising firm. Orwell is not saying that working for an advertising firm is the best sort of life (he is not saying that the whole commercial world against which Gordon revolted is a good world); but he is saying that it is better than not working at all, being cold and half-starved, pretending to be writing poetry and not really writing anything. Lewis, however, refuses to see this in the novel and paraphrases it in a vein of cheap mockery: ". . . Rosemary trips in, snuggles down beside him in the buggy bed. . . . When the little stranger is announced, the turning point comes. . . ."[51] The point of the novel is that there *is* a turning point. Gordon reaches it and recognizes that the healthy and intelligent man does as much as he can with his life, whatever the state of the world or his own society at the time, instead of cursing the whole thing to hell. Perceiving that the framework is faulty, he will seek to correct it, but meanwhile he makes the best of the framework. If he flees from it, he flees from the only world there is, and he diminishes himself.

In *Keep the Aspidistra Flying* Orwell is working in the tradition of the early Arnold Bennett, and the difference between Orwell's and Bennett's handling of the same subject indicates not only Orwell's healthiness but also his relatively optimistic view. Bennett's first novel, *A Man from the North*, is, like *Keep the Aspidistra Flying*, the story of a London clerk with literary ambitions. Richard Larch no more enjoys his work with a firm of solicitors than Gordon Comstock enjoys his work with the advertising agency; but he keeps his job and, giving it only half of his mind, he does so well that he is promoted to the position of head clerk. He fails, however, to publish even so much as Gordon does. Convinced that he will never make a writer, discouraged and lonely, he marries a lower-middle-class girl and settles for a commercial career. Now, whereas Orwell regards his hero's life as reasonably successful, Bennett does not. The tone of *A Man from the North* is the detached one of naturalism—the style is remarkably like that of Maugham's first novel, *Liza of Lambeth,* published a year earlier—but it is clear that Bennett regards Richard's story as more miserable in its way than Liza's. The conclusion of Maugham's novel is Liza's death in childbirth; the conclusion of Bennett's is a life-in-death for Richard.

V. S. Pritchett does not share Rosenfeld's belief that Orwell consciously intended to kill himself when he retired to the Scottish island. Still, says Pritchett, the retirement killed him; and if he was not consciously seeking death, he was quite consciously seeking punishment. To Pritchett the flight to the island is a gesture almost as extravagant as it is to Rosenfeld. If, however, Orwell was deliberately rejecting all of the comforts and luxuries that the royalties of his books could buy to live like less fortunate people, he was doing something that he would not have done before. (It seems more likely that he wished, like George Bowling, to come up for air, to get away from the modern world for a little while.) True, he was passionately concerned with the plight of the poor. For months he shared the lives of the most poverty-stricken miners in the North of England, eating their food, sleeping in their dirty, crowded bedrooms, and even going down into the mines with them because he felt a moral obligation to learn how they lived in the only way that he could thoroughly learn. But he did not feel obliged to spend the rest of his life with them. "It is a kind of duty," he said in *The Road to Wigan Pier,* "to see and smell such places, especially to smell them, lest you forget that they exist; though perhaps it is better not to stay too long."[52] The time that he spent as a dishwasher and tramp, which he writes about in *Down and Out in Paris and London,* was partly a kind of penance for having been a member of the Indian Imperial Police in Burma and therefore an instrument of the imperialism that he had come to detest. But when he put behind him his life with the dregs of French society and the pariahs of English society, he no longer felt (he says in *The Road to Wigan Pier*) the guilt which he had once felt about helping to oppress the Burmese.

The truth is that the sensationalism, the extravagance, the suicidal tendencies that Pritchett and Rosenfeld attribute to Orwell fit him very badly. If he had not already learned it elsewhere, Orwell learned from the poor the stoicism he admired, a stoicism without any pretense to the heroic. If the average person were to work as hard as Orwell did in the period covered by *Down and Out in Paris and London,* he would regard himself as something prodigious, and with good reason. Orwell, however, waves aside his constitution-wrecking routine to tell of a girl he knew who worked in a bistro from seven in the morning until midnight every day for a whole year. Moreover, Orwell not only survived the *Down and Out* period; he even got some satisfaction from it besides the moral satisfaction. There is one scene in the book in a comparatively comfortable flophouse which has the raffish expansiveness and jolliness of similar scenes in Joyce Cary's *The Horse's Mouth.* When, however, the flophouses are filthy, there is nothing sensational in Orwell's descriptions of them, just as there is nothing sensational in his description of the charity ward of the large Paris hospital where he was not so much treated as ignored. George Bowling's account of World War I does not contain the parades of horror that are to be found in the average "war novel." Writing of his own experiences in Spain, Orwell admits, with his usual candor, that war sometimes has its attractions: ". . . the guns on the open trucks making one's heart leap as guns always do, and reviving the pernicious feeling, so difficult to get rid of, that war *is* glorious after all."[53] But Orwell no more makes war romantic, as Evelyn Waugh made it later, than he makes it horrible, as Richard Aldington had made it earlier. Like other soldiers, he says, he spent most of his time trying to keep warm and killing lice. He was, in fact, nearly killed himself (a bullet went through his throat, just missing the trachea), but he makes no commotion over his wound. Here, as elsewhere when he writes about himself, there is an objectivity like that in the writings of doctors who, for the sake of science, have reported their own symptoms in the impersonal terms of the medical dictionary.

There is, to be sure, something of Kafka's atmosphere in the last pages of *Homage to Catalonia*, where Orwell rushes back and forth in the Spanish War Department Building, looking for an officer who can get him the letter without which his friend Kopp will certainly be shot: the labyrinth of corridors, the glimpses into rooms where people are drawing up heaven knows what orders, the hands of the clock moving towards closing time, Orwell's struggle to make himself understood in his limited Spanish, his voice almost giving out because of his recent wound in the throat. But the nightmare was not too much for Orwell. He got the letter for Kopp.

iii. THE EXCURSIONS INTO POVERTY

The evidence so far has indicated the comprehensiveness and strength of Orwell's rebellion. The examination of further evidence will show, I believe, the equal comprehensiveness and strength of the responsibility with which the rebellion was paradoxically combined.

In the first place, Orwell's responsibility is demonstrated by his investigations of poverty. His initial investigation may seem at first sight to indicate neurosis rather than responsibility, and it may as well be admitted that the original impulse behind the investigation was a strong emotional one. He had just returned from Burma on leave, and, having got away from his policeman's job, he resolved never to return and resigned his post. Even before he left Burma, he had begun to feel that guilt which, he said, all Anglo-Indians felt, and which the police felt particularly since they were "part of the actual machinery of despotism."[54] He thought that he had to get away for a time not only from imperialism, but from "every form of man's dominion over man."[55] Once he had been accepted by the people who live at the bottom of society, at least part of his guilt (he believed) would be absolved. Feelings of guilt and acts of penance, however, are not invariably neurotic. Besides, it should be noted that Orwell did his penance for only a short time. He did not feel obliged to spend the rest of his life in expiation of his tour of duty in Burma.

Moreover, Orwell's penance was partly involuntary. Before his initial experience of poverty was over, he had got more than he had bargained for. When, however, he found himself even poorer than he had planned to be, he did not whine about his hunger and discomfort. Nor did he complain when circumstances compelled him to become not only one of the poorest people of Paris, but also one of the hardest working of the Paris poor. Instead of wishing that he had gone no further than hobnobbing with the workers in bars on payday, he welcomed the opportunity of working with them through the week. For he realized then that, since their lives consisted mostly of work, to work with them was the only satisfactory way to learn how they lived. (Similarly, he later chose not only to drink with English miners in the pubs and live with them in their boarding houses, but also to go down in the mines with them.)

Orwell made his first excursion into poverty in the Rue Coq d'Or in Paris. Between the thirty-six francs that he got from giving English lessons and the bit of money that he made from an occasional newspaper article, together with resorts to his small savings in emergencies, he lived more or less in the manner of the average poor person in the district. When his savings had dwindled to two hundred and fifty francs, he knew that he would have to get another job to manage to live even thus well. But just as he was casting about for work, his room was robbed and his savings were taken. Now he had only six francs a day (provided he was lucky and no pupils cancelled their lessons), a smaller amount than most people in the slum had to live on. He had touched bottom with a vengeance.

A less responsible writer than Orwell might have turned such an experience of poverty into melodrama. Orwell, however, writes the sort of documentary that he was to write about similar experiences later. He describes, for instance, his constant evasions of the shopkeepers who would ask him why he no longer patronized them, the visits to the pawnshop, the physical and psychological results of a bread and margarine diet.

After some weeks of near-starvation Orwell got a job as a *plongeur* in a large hotel. He worked from eleven to fourteen hours a day in a temperature which often reached one hundred and twenty degrees, and his duties included

> making tea, coffee and chocolate, fetching meals from the kitchen, wines from the cellar and fruit and so forth from the dining-room, slicing bread, making toast, rolling pats of butter, measuring jam, opening milk cans, counting lumps of sugar, boiling eggs, cooking porridge, pounding ice, grinding coffee—all this for from a hundred to two hundred customers.[56]

In addition to all these jobs, he waited on the waiters, cleaned up after everyone, and washed dishes.

In a short while Orwell was able to adapt himself almost completely to the *plongeur's* way of life: on six days a week, back-breaking work and just enough sleep to get by; on the seventh, drinks in the bistro and plenty of sleep. It was a life rather like that of a beast that works in the fields all day, is well fed at night (if the hotel worked its employees hard, at least it allowed them decent rations of food and wine), and falls asleep immediately. In the routine of such a life there is little time or energy left for thought, and the average *plongeur* simply lives from one day to the next without reflecting upon the conditions under which he spends his days. (Work is the opium of people like *plongeurs*.) It would not be altogether a bad life for a man who merely wished an escape from himself, an escape from society, an oblivion. Orwell's sense of responsibility, however, did not allow him to slip into an animal unconsciousness or an animal contentment. Hard as he had to work, he managed not only to live the life of a drudge, but also to think about it, to consider the position of the *plongeur* in the hierarchy of the big hotel (at the very bottom) and in society, too. He may not have got all of the right answers, but he asked some of the right questions. Why, he asked himself, should there be *plongeurs* in the first place? The usual explanation is that they do a job which, however disagreeable and arduous it may be, is necessary, like that of a coal miner or a sewer worker. Actually, Orwell says, the *plongeur* does not do anything necessary or even useful. The luxury he provides is really not much of a luxury. Like the man who pulls the rickshaw, he does an incredible amount of work for a silly sort of smartness. (Orwell argues, moreover, that in the running of a big hotel more important things, including cleanliness, must be sacrificed to smartness: ". . . we saved time by being dirty."[57]

Then Orwell suggests another reason for the existence of *plongeurs* and others whom he calls the serfs of the modern world: a middle-class fear of the mob.

> A *plongeur* is a slave, and a wasted slave, doing stupid and largely unnecessary work. He is kept at work, ultimately, because of a vague feeling that he would be dangerous if he had leisure. And educated people, who should be on his side, acquiesce in the process, because they know nothing about him and consequently are afraid of him. I say this of the *plongeur* because it is his case I have been considering; it would apply equally to numberless other types of worker.[58]

From his job in the large hotel Orwell went to one in a small restaurant, where the hours were even longer (over fifteen a day) and the work was even more exhausting. Besides, the owner, who had opened the business without sufficient capital and had debts everywhere, was paying Orwell only a fraction of his wages each week. Orwell wrote to a friend in England, asking him to get him a job there; when the friend replied that he had got him a job taking care of what he called a tame imbecile, Orwell quit the restaurant and crossed the Channel. Arriving in London, however, he learned that the tame imbecile had been taken abroad for a month. Of the money that his London friend had sent him for passage and other expenses Orwell had only nineteen shillings left.

Orwell's method of making the nineteen shillings stretch over a period of several weeks may seem outlandish, and his explanations for choosing this method may seem inconsistent. But before assuming that Orwell was slightly mad, one should remember that he was still a young man; that he had not lived in England since leaving Eton; that he realized how ignorant he was of the social problems of his own country; that he was naturally confused; and that he was trying to learn a lot about himself and about society in a hurry, in an urgency of responsibility.

Orwell made his nineteen shillings last for some weeks by going on the bum. The first reason he gives for doing this instead of borrowing more money is that it did not seem decent to ask his friend for more money. The second reason is that he wanted to get in touch with the English working classes. ". . . I knew nothing about working-class conditions. . . . When I thought of poverty I thought of it in terms of brute starvation. Therefore my mind turned towards the extreme cases: tramps, beggars, criminals, prostitutes. . . ."[59] The third reason is that he wanted to get away from the respectable world. There is probably yet another reason for Orwell's going on the bum instead of borrowing money. There seems to have been a sort of Robinson Crusoe side of him which preferred to see how far his own resources would carry him when his possessions were reduced to a minimum.

The Robinson Crusoe impulse, however, like the reluctance to borrow money, was probably subordinate to the other two reasons, the wish to get away from the respectable world and the wish to get in touch with the poor. Orwell thought that by going on the road he would get to know the poor of his own country as he had got to know the poor of Paris—from the inside.

To enter the world of the casual laborer and the tramp took all of Orwell's courage.

> One evening . . . I set out and wandered eastward until I landed up at a common lodging-house in Limehouse Causeway. It was a dark, dirty-looking place. . . . Heavens, how I had to screw up

> my courage before I went in! It seems ridiculous now. But you
> see I was still half-afraid of the working class. I wanted to get
> in touch with them . . . but I still thought of them as alien and
> dangerous.[60]

Orwell went into the lodging-house expecting a fight, and, in fact,
a stevedore—very large and very drunk—came reeling at him. "He
lurched towards me with a broad red face thrust out and a dan-
gerous-looking fishy gleam in his eyes. I stiffened my self. . . . The
next moment the stevedore . . . flung his arms around my neck
' 'Ave a cup of tea, chum!' he cried . . . ."[61]

Staying in the alien world was a more severe test of Orwell's sense
of responsibility than entering it was. The men he met in it presented something which, to a middle-class man like Orwell, was worse
than danger: dirtiness. In spite of the cordial reception by the
stevedore, Orwell found the first night in a common lodging-house a
pretty shocking experience, and the first morning inspection in a
casual ward an even more shocking one. A tramp's clothes, he says,
are bad enough, but they cover up even worse things. Nevertheless,
Orwell overcame the natural squeamishness of the middle-class
man, and he remained long enough among casual laborers and
tramps to learn what they were really like. In the last part of
Down and Out he attempts to teach the British public what he has
learned.

Tramps are not dangerous, lazy, or larcenous; they are simply
pitiable. They are what they are by force of circumstances. If they
are dirty, it is not because they enjoy being dirty, but because they
have no way to wash. If they are dull and abject, it is not because
they are stupid and unmanly, but because they are chronically
undernourished. The usual explanations of why tramps take to the
road are, says Orwell, just silly. Some people say that they do so
to steal; some say that they do so to avoid work; one sociologist
says that tramps are atavistic (about as sensible, Orwell remarks,
as saying that traveling salesmen are atavistic). The only reason that
the typical tramp goes on the road is that he must tramp or starve.
He cannot stay in one parish, but must go from casual ward to
casual ward. Remember, says Orwell, that the tramp is an Englishman out of work, and you will quit thinking of him as a monster.

The tramp, then, is not a public enemy, but a public victim. As
a responsible member of the British public, Orwell feels obliged

to seek some remedy for the conditions under which tramps are living and to put that remedy before his readers. The question, he says, is what to do with hungry, idle men, and the obvious answer is to let them grow their own food. Each workhouse should run a small farm, and tramps should be allowed to stay at one workhouse for a month—or a year—if there is work for them to do on the farm, instead of being pushed from one to another night after night. Until this new system is set up, Orwell suggests a compulsory improvement of lodging-houses, so that they will provide decent quarters for the men who must stay in them, not gold mines for their owners.

iv. THE PERCEPTION OF RELIGIOUS VALUES

Further evidence of the responsibility of Orwell's rebellion is provided by his attitude toward religion. I have already shown that Orwell regarded the churches as reactionary and puritanic, that he had a low opinion of the clergy generally, and that the whole make-up of his mind and his emotions was unreligious. This, however, is only half of the truth. The other half is that Orwell was honest enough to admit the fact that, although organized religion might be an impediment to the kind of social progress which he desired, it was also an impediment to certain kinds of social change which he recoiled from: the rootlessness and the ruthlessness of much of modern life. This second side of Orwell's ambivalent attitude produces passages which, taken in isolation, would seem to put him right in the religious camp. Speaking of life in the communities which have grown up around the light industry in the South of England, he says: "It is a rather restless, cultureless life . . . in which children grow up with an intimate knowledge of magnetos and in complete ignorance of the Bible."[62] Discussing the civilization of nineteenth-century America, he says that its good morale was based at least partly on unthinking piety. The gist of "Decline of the English Murder" is that morals, too, are best founded on religious feelings, if only those of fear, or at least upon feelings which pay tribute—as vice does to virtue—to religious ones. The title of the essay is, of course, ironical; the incidence of murder is not lower than it was in the nineteenth century, but higher; it is the importance of murder that has declined. Murder is committed more casually and read about with greater boredom than anybody would have imagined possible a hundred years ago. It is difficult to believe, says Orwell, that the most widely discussed English murder of the forties "will be so long remembered as the old domestic poisoning dramas, products of a stable society where the all-prevailing hypocrisy did at least ensure that crimes as serious as murder should have strong emotion behind them."[63]

Orwell is not a sceptic recommending religion as Voltaire did —because if others believed, he would be less likely to have his silver stolen or his throat cut. Besides this merely preventive value of religion, he recognizes a positive value, especially to a certain kind of temperament. Dorothy Hare, the heroine of *A Clergyman's Daughter,* is an example of such a temperament. The religious community

which Orwell treats so satirically in *A Clergyman's Daughter* is
ultimately a background for the story of Dorothy. This is, among
other things, the story of a woman who does a fantastic amount of
work. In addition to the household responsibilities, like the butcher's bill, she has all the responsibilities connected with the fabric
of the church, since her father will not bother his head about them.
The sexton comes to her about leaking roofs, broken pews, missing
hymn books, smashed windows, torn cassocks. She also makes all of
the parish calls that a curate would make if her father could spare
enough from his speculation on the stock market to keep one. To
perform her innumerable duties, Dorothy puts in seventeen hours
on an average day. The novel begins as Dorothy begins her day,
bathing and dressing with lightning speed so that she can do half
a dozen jobs before she goes to Holy Communion. Eighty pages
later Orwell is describing what she does after a full morning of
domestic and religious duties.

> She had had an exhausting afternoon, starting off with ten miles
> or so of bicycling to and fro in the sun, delivering the parish
> magazine.   After tea Dorothy had dashed up to the church to
> put fresh flowers on the altar, and then she had typed out her
> father's sermon—her typewriter was a rickety pre-Boer "Invincible,"
> on which you couldn't average eight hundred words an hour—and
> after supper she had weeded the pea rows until the light failed
> and her back seemed to be breaking.[64]

At this point she stops to talk for an hour to Mr. Warburton, the
parish lecher, after which she feels guilty, not because of the company she has kept, but because of the time she has wasted. Then she
returns to the rectory to work half the night on costumes for a
church pageant.

As though her life were not hard enough, Dorothy imposes upon
herself all sorts of austerities and mortifications. She takes cold
baths, eats no bacon at breakfast, pushes aside the hassock and
kneels on the bare stones of the church. When she catches herself
not attending to prayers or looking vainly at the pleats which she
has put in her father's surplice, she takes a pin from her lapel and
jabs her forearm hard enough to draw blood. In one church scene
she is obliged to assign herself a special penance. She is so revolted
by the appearance of an old lady (whom Orwell describes in sufficiently revolting terms) that she forgets for a few moments why she

is in church. When she remembers, she is appalled at the idea of drinking from the Communion cup after the old lady. Then she sees through an open door a ray of sunlight on the leaves of a lime tree, and the love of God, the power of worship, her peace of mind return to her.

> O all ye green things upon the earth, praise ye the Lord! She began to pray, ardently, joyfully, thankfully. The wafer melted upon her tongue. She took the chalice from her father, and tasted without repulsion, even with an added joy in this small act of self-abasement, the wet imprint of Miss Mayfill's lips on its silver rim.[65]

Although natural beauty has enabled Dorothy to pray on this occasion and prompts her to pray on others, she feels scruples about her responses to nature. Once, on her parish rounds, she stops in a field full of the sounds and odors of summer, and she prays with such passion that she forgets herself. When she becomes aware of herself again, she is kissing a frond of fennel, and she feels guilty of paganism.

In view of her scruples, her mortifications, and her overwork, it is no wonder that Dorothy suffers an attack of amnesia. She finds herself in the London streets and, bewildered and having nothing else to do, she joins some hop-pickers on their way to Kent. At this point Orwell cannot resist doing a documentary: hops and the people who pick them take over the story while Dorothy's memory is in abeyance. Shortly before the end of the hop-picking season a shock restores Dorothy's memory. She goes to London, runs out of money, and lives for a time in the streets. Orwell documents the life of the homeless woman in London in the manner of *Down and Out* (with the exception of one adventure—the winter night that Dorothy spends in Trafalgar Square—which is rendered as a dramatic scene and rises to a kind of nightmare). Dorothy is eventually jailed for begging, bailed out by her cousin's valet, and given a job as a schoolmistress.

The school section gives Orwell another opportunity for yet another documentary, but this time the documentary does not take the story away from Dorothy. The fraudulent school which Orwell exposes serves—as did the parish which he satirized—to exhibit the unselfishness of Dorothy. She realizes that she is so inexperienced that she will have to educate herself before she can educate anyone else, but she resolves to do whatever energy and will can do to save the children from the swindle which the owner of the school practices upon them. The fact that the owner starves and bullies her does not divert her from her resolution. In her dedication to the girls she forgets her own comfort and health; she spends her miserable salary on books and equipment for her classroom. As the girls begin to respond to her teaching (formerly they had been virtually anesthetized by a routine of penmanship and rote learning), Dorothy feels that she would be glad to go on teaching, even at ten shillings a week and her keep, for the rest of her life. She thinks that she has found her vocation. Indeed, Dorothy turns out to be such a good teacher, that the owner—whose notion of a good schoolmistress is one who exerts herself chiefly in stealing pupils from other schools —fires her. Shortly after she is fired, her father forgives her (the scandal which her disappearance has given rise to has been discredited and, besides, her father needs her to run the house). And so Dorothy returns to her first vocation.

But she has lost her faith. And this, she says, is the most horrible thing that has happened to her. In comparison to the loss of faith, the lack of money, the hunger, the loneliness are nothing. She has no God to pray to and to thank, and nothing in the universe will ever be the same again. At this point of the story the dimension of Orwell's sympathy which is least expected appears. Even though Orwell was not religious himself, it is not surprising that he would admire someone who worked as hard for religion as Dorothy does, since he admired hard work. He could understand the penances that she assigned herself, because he had once imposed penance on himself. And he would naturally be on Dorothy's side, whatever her convictions were, since she was the underdog in her father's house, in the streets, and in the school. Less predictable than all this is Orwell's remarkable insight into Dorothy's problem of faith.

Some of the things that she once believed, Dorothy tells Mr. Warburton, were difficult to believe; some, now that she looks back on them, were silly. Nevertheless, the fact remains that she has nothing to put in the place of the things that she once believed in. Warburton's reply to Dorothy's problem is, in effect, then put nothing. Now, Warburton, with his complacent atheism, is certainly a more attractive character than the Rector, with his faith. Among other things he is, in his way, kind to Dorothy, whereas her father is cruel. A novelist writing a mere anti-religious story would set the two men up as the poles of the story and cause Dorothy to be drawn from the one to the other in the course of the action. In *A Clergyman's Daughter*, however, what is ultimately important is not the difference between Warburton and the Rector, but the difference between Warburton and Dorothy. Warburton, says Orwell, "was quite incapable of realizing how a mind naturally pious must recoil from a world discovered to be meaningless."[66]

Orwell not only recognizes the value of religious belief; he recognizes the cheapness of the sort of belief which much of the modern world has put in its place. In her teaching period, for instance, Dorothy hears of a school in which there is a daily recitation of this sort of catechism:

Q. What is the secret of success?
A. The secret of success is efficiency.
Q. What is the test of efficiency?
A. The test of efficiency is success.[67]

Dorothy concludes that there is no replacement for faith. If you have faith, if you can serve God, nothing else matters, nothing can dismay you, your whole life is illuminated by its ultimate purpose. If you do not have faith, the world is a grey and desolate place, and you feel the pointlessness of your life like a physical pang in your heart.

Dorothy is still wrestling with the problem as she makes ready to complete the costumes for the church pageant on which she was working when she left the rectory. "Lord, I believe," she prays, "help Thou my unbelief."[68] At that moment the smell of burning glue comes to her nostrils, and she jumps from her chair to run to the stove and add the water which, in her abstraction, she has forgot. Then she looks at the clock and, reproaching herself for having wasted twenty minutes, throws herself heart and soul into the costume-making.

> The problem of faith and no faith had vanished utterly from her mind. It was beginning to get dark, but, too busy to stop and light the lamp, she worked on, pasting strip after strip into place, with absorbed pious concentration, in the penetrating smell of the gluepot.[69]

The burning glue, says Orwell, was the answer to Dorothy's prayer. But a distraction is not much of an answer; the smell of burning glue is no substitute for the odor of sanctity. Orwell, however, can provide nothing better.

When, earlier, Dorothy tells Mr. Warburton that she has lost her faith but that she still intends to take up her old way of life and her old responsibilities, Warburton says that she is one of the "Anglican atheists" who make the worst of both worlds. "You stick to the Christian scheme of things, but you leave Paradise out of it."[70] Christianity without Paradise is, in fact, Orwell's prescription for the ills of the modern world. In his essay on Arthur Koestler Orwell says that Koestler has a picture of the future as an earthly paradise, but that he also has another picture of it as a totalitarian hell. And so he trusts to a quasi-religious solution: everything is in dreadful shape now, but all will come right in the end. But most thinking people, says Orwell, doubt that men's problems can ever be solved. Without religious belief, however, the idea that men's problems will never be solved is intolerable. The trouble is that very few people (Orwell considered) have any religious beliefs. "The real problem is how to restore the religious attitude while accepting death as final. Men can only be happy when they do not assume that the object of life is happiness."[71]

Dorothy Hare is able to combine the religious attitude with an acceptance of death as final, but she is not restoring; she is substituting. She can work with pious concentration on the costumes for the pageant and bring an almost saintly dedication to the girls' school because her attitude is religious to start with. Orwell is aware of the fact, and the fact was for him one of the most significant in the modern world, that for those who start without religion the dedication and the piety are difficult, if not impossible.

Whether or not the restoration of the religious attitude is in any way possible, Orwell's remarks on it in the Koestler essay and in *A Clergyman's Daughter* qualify his hostile writing on religion and illustrate another aspect of his responsibility. Unsympathetic to organized religion, Orwell nevertheless believed it to be a vehicle of values which might in time disappear from the Western World. The leaven in his final recipe for a better world is religion; his statements about the necessity for following that recipe are the paradoxical kind upon which G. K. Chesterton constructed *Orthodoxy*.

v. THE ENGAGEMENT IN POLITICS

Just as Orwell's scorn of churches and clergymen did not prevent him from being responsible in religious matters, his scorn of government and political parties did not prevent him from being responsible in political ones. Refusing to espouse any of the orthodoxies that were thrust upon him, he went out of his way to embrace what he thought was his duty. "I suggest," he said,

> that we should draw a sharper distinction than we do at present between our political and our literary loyalties, and should recognize that a willingness to *do* certain necessary but distasteful things does not carry with it any obligation to swallow the beliefs that usually go with them.[72]

The writer who accepts any political discipline, whether of the right or of the left, compromises his literary integrity. Yet writers, like other men, must engage in politics. They must see the fallacy of supposing that one cause is no better than another because they are advanced by the same bad means.

It was his ability to distinguish between causes on the one hand and the means by which they are advanced and the doctrines by which they are accompanied on the other, that enabled Orwell to cut through the confusion of the pacifist issue. While the super-patriots cried my country right or wrong and the pacifists cried that war was always wrong, Orwell pointed out that war was wrong but that it was also necessary. He was sufficiently aware of the horror of war to understand how a man might be tempted to say in desperation that one side is as bad as the other and that he is therefore going to be neutral. Yet one must not, said Orwell, remain neutral, since there is no such thing as a war in which it does not matter who is the victor.

It was because he believed that English intellectuals on the whole took an irresponsible attitude toward World War II that Orwell quarreled bitterly with them during the War years. None of them, he said, exactly wished the Axis Powers to win the War. But many of them were rather pleased when various Allied campaigns went badly and England was humiliated, and they hoped that Russia rather than the United States and England would smash the Axis.* To take this sort of attitude, Orwell thought, one first has to take leave of his senses, or at least of reality, as one has to take leave of them to believe (for example) that American troops were brought to England, not to fight the Germans, but to put down an English revolution. Only an intellectual, Orwell said, would believe such stuff; an ordinary man could not possibly be such a fool. Hence, although he criticized the government for its sweeping suspicions of intellectuals, he also attacked that wide segment of intellectuals of whom the government did well to be suspicious. Even as late as 1943, he thought, a great many of them were unaware of some of the most obvious facts of the War. They did not have to be defeatist or treasonable to be dangerous. They were dangerous because they were completely unrealistic. Instead of attending to political and military facts, they followed intellectual fashions. Orwell seemed to think that these fashions sometimes had as little relation to the shape of the real world as women's fashions sometimes have to women's figures.

For instance, he believed that the disparity between intellectual fashion and the events of the actual world was in part responsible for the pessimism of the twenties. The twenties were pessimistic precisely because they were exceptionally comfortable. When people are hungry, they do not despair of the universe, or even bother their heads about it. In the twenties, however, the War had been won, the dictators had not yet appeared, the puritanism that had cramped the pre-war years was in retreat, and everybody had hopes of getting rich quickly, if he was not already rich. Disenchantment became fashionable.

No doubt this explanation oversimplifies the twenties; on the thirties, however, Orwell is more convincing. For the intellectuals of that time were often about as real in their political thought as a child is in a game of cowboys and Indians. Some of them talked (just like Frank Illidge in *Point Counter Point*) of the necessity of political murder. What enabled them to talk so nonchalantly about killing people was, of course, that (like Illidge until Spandrell

---

* In the interval between the Russo-German pact of nonaggression and the invasion of Russia by Germany, Orwell was extremely unpopular with English writers who followed the Party line. One of his poems describes his experience with the cult of Russia in the United Kingdom. When, in 1940, he said that he would fight to keep the Germans out of England, one of the replies consisted of four pages explaining why his sentiment was a treasonable one. Loving one's country, Orwell said in the poem, had become the blackest sort of crime.

thrust facts in the face of his theories) they had never seen a man killed, much less killed one themselves. As an example, he quotes from Auden's "Spain." He admires the poem on the whole ("one of the few decent things that have been written about the Spanish war"), but he says that the line about the necessity of murder could have been written only by a man to whom murder was no more than a word. "Personally I would not speak so lightly of murder. . . . I have seen the bodies of numbers of murdered men—I don't mean killed in battle, I mean murdered. Therefore I have some conception of what murder means—the terror, the hatred, the howling relatives, the post-mortems, the blood, the smells."[73] (It should be mentioned that in later revisions of "Spain" Auden speaks of murder as a fact, not a necessity.) Similarly, it was because they had no first-hand knowledge of purges, summary trials and executions, and the other instruments of the police state that writers of the thirties were able to pipe up for Russia.

Orwell's writings about war, both his account of his own experiences in the Spanish Civil War and his observations about World Wars I and II, offer further testimony to his sense of responsibility. He went to Spain to write newspaper articles about the War, but instead he enlisted with the Republican forces. After describing conditions in Barcelona in December, 1936, he says: ". . . I recognized it immediately as a state of affairs worth fighting for."[74]

Of course, other writers besides Orwell fought the Fascists in Spain, and their reasons for doing so may sound like Orwell's. "You know how I feel about the importance of democratic freedom," Christopher Caudwell said in explanation of his enlisting in the British Battalion of the International Brigade. "The Spanish People's Army needs help badly; their struggle, if they fail, will certainly be ours tomorrow, and, believing as I do, it seems clear where my duty lies."[75] But whereas Orwell is talking about his feelings after arriving in Spain, Caudwell is talking about his feelings before arriving. Orwell is responding to an actual experience; Caudwell, an orthodox Marxist who wrote a book attacking the new physics because it contradicted Marxist materialism and determinism, is fitting an event into a theoretical system.

Caudwell did not live to write a book about the Spanish Civil War (he was killed two months after he enlisted), but the reports on the war that did get written were frequently exercises in arranging facts to fit theories, so that the War became for many a struggle between good Republicans and bad Fascists—or vice-versa. Orwell, however, uncommitted to any party, does not deal in shatterproof stereotypes and abstractions. Even a minor episode in his account illustrates this. Early in his combat experience he saw a soldier, probably carrying a message, dashing along the parapet of a Fascist trench; the soldier was only half-dressed, and he held up his trousers with both hands as he ran. He was in easy range of Orwell's rifle, but Orwell did not fire at him. "I had come here to shoot at 'Fascists'; but a man who is holding up his trousers isn't a 'Fascist,' he is visibly a fellow-creature, similar to yourself, and you don't feel like shooting a him."[76] However reluctant he was, Orwell's reflections on this occasion did not cause him to throw away his rifle, or even to make a habit of not shooting at the enemy.

Wyndham Lewis questions Orwell's motives for joining the Republican militia. "It was, of course, a *sensational* decision, not an act of reason. His boyish sporting instinct 'recognized immediately' that it would be great fun to be a 'militiaman.' "[77] To Lewis, Orwell is a sort of modern Robert Louis Stevenson, not (as one might suspect) because he led an active and productive life in spite of illness, but because he was a Scottish romantic. Actually, Orwell never exploited the romantic side of his Spanish adventures; in fact, he always played it down. If he was a man on the spot in Spain because of Scottish romanticism, he wrote about his Spanish experiences, as he did about his others, with English understatement.

But Lewis is not content with reading the Rover Boy into Orwell; he also reads into him something sinister: "Had Orwell been of German nationality who can doubt that he would have been an S.S. man?"[78] This remark seems a perfect illustration of the irresponsibility with which Orwell charged many British intellectuals. Orwell no more had the viciousness of the Nazi than he had the naiveté of the Boy Scout. And there was something else that made him the least likely of candidates for totalitarian parties or armies: his refusal to allow himself to be turned into a robot. He quotes with approval E. M. Forster's comment on *Prufrock* and other early poems of Eliot that he read in 1917:

> They sang of private disgust and diffidence, and of people who seemed genuine because they were unattractive or weak. . . . Here

was a protest . . . and the more congenial for being feeble. . . .
He who could turn aside to complain of ladies and drawing rooms
preserved a tiny drop of our self-respect, he carried on the human
heritage.[79]

Orwell's reply to some scornful remarks of Louis MacNeice on
the Forster passage is that Forster knew what World War I was
like and that MacNeice barely remembered it (the inexperience of
the intellectual speaking again). And then he adds his own agree-
ment with Forster on Eliot: "What a relief it would have been at
such a time, to read about the hesitations of a middle-aged high-
brow. . . . After the bombs and the food-queues and the recruiting
posters, a human voice! What a relief!"[80] Because he is fighting for
his country, the soldier does not have to cease thinking with his
own head. Because he cares about his country, the civilian
need not confine his reading to propaganda or believe all the
propaganda that he reads. But neither should he, with the in-
genuousness of the pacifist or the cynicism of the disaffected, take
the line that all propaganda stories are lies simply because they are
propaganda stories. Orwell sounds a cynical warning against cynicism: The Japanese and German atrocities really happened, he says,
even though Lord Halifax said that they happened.

Orwell knew just how dreadful war was, and he was sensitive
enough to be revolted by the horrors of some aspects of life in the
Republican forces even before he got into combat: "Here we are
. . . defending Democracy against Fascism . . . and the detail of our
lives is just as sordid and degrading as it could be in prison. . . ."[81]
But he also realized that the fact that the soldier who is fighting
for liberty and the preservation of civilized life must give up his
personal liberty and the amenities of civilized life is one of the
paradoxes that any sensible man must accept. But some people have
become (because of their good fortune to live in the safety and se-
curity of a democracy) "too civilized to grasp the obvious. . . . To
survive you often have to fight, and to fight you have to dirty yourself. War is evil and it is often the lesser evil."[82]

Orwell's responsibility is exhibited yet again in that area where
questions of politics and morals are most closely involved with
questions of language and literature, first in his observations of
the writings of others, and second in his own writing. Like many
other observers, Orwell believed that the English language (along

with other languages) was deteriorating. Unlike many others, he thought that it was possible to do more than just watch it get worse.

> Now it is clear that the decline of a language must ultimately have political and economic causes; it is not due simply to the bad influence of this or that individual writer.   But an effect can become a cause, reinforcing the original cause and producing the same effect in an intensified form, and so on indefinitely. A man may take to drink because he feels himself a failure, and then fail all the more completely because he drinks.   It is rather the same thing that is happening to the English language.   It becomes ugly and inaccurate because our thoughts are foolish, but the slovenliness of our language makes it easier to have foolish thoughts.   The point is that the process is reversible.   Modern English, especially written English, is full of bad habits which spread by imitation and which can be avoided if one is willing to take the necessary trouble.   If one gets rid of these habits one can think more clearly, and to think more clearly is a necessary first step towards political regeneration: so that the fight against bad English is not frivolous and is not the exclusive concern of professional writers.[83]

Like contemporary prose generally, political writing (Orwell observed) is full of bad metaphors, pretentious diction, and downright meaningless words. Because they do not really think about what they are saying, writers on politics not only mix metaphors, but twist them quite out of their original meaning. For example, they write *toe the line* as *tow the line;* they speak of *the hammer and the anvil* with the implication that it is the hammer that breaks the anvil. It is not ignorance, absent-mindedness, or indifference, however, but deliberate intent to deceive that produces certain other abuses of language. Pretentious words like *phenomenon, categorical, utilize,* and *objective* are used to make simple statements sound impressive and to make biased judgments look impartial. Adjectives like *epoch-making, inevitable,* and *historical* are used to cover the most indefensible acts of power politics. Marxist jargon like *hangman, petty bourgeois,* and *White Guard* is used to discredit opponents of innumerable complexions. Words like *socialism, freedom,* and *patriotic* are used in a context in which they have no meaning at all. Modifiers are attached to verbs to make phrases like *render inoperative, militate against,* and *give rise to,* while simple verbs like *break, spoil,* and *kill* are eliminated.

Political prose, then (Orwell believed) was less likely to debate an issue with an opponent or describe a situation than to browbeat the opposition or obscure a situation. For instance, a British intellectual who wishes to defend Russian totalitarianism cannot come out in the open and say plainly that he believes in the policy of killing political opponents when it gets results, but he can say (Orwell suggests) something like this:

> While freely conceding that the Soviet regime exhibits certain features which the humanitarian may be inclined to deplore, we must, I think, agree that a certain curtailment of the right to political opposition is an unavoidable concomitant of transitional periods, and that the rigors which the Russian people have been called upon to undergo have been amply justified in the sphere of concrete achievement.[84]

Since the political messes in which we find ourselves are partly the result of the decay of language, it is possible, says Orwell, to do something about politics by doing something about language. One cannot, of course, reform in a day a kind of language which is "designed to make lies sound truthful and murder respectable, and to give an appearance of solidity to pure wind,"[85] but one can at least write clearly and simply himself about politics. He will then have avoided the follies and vices common to all political camps, or at least the worst ones. Since he will not be speaking in any of the partisan jargons, his stupid and false remarks will be obvious, even to himself.

Orwell was aware that his own prose was not always an absolute model of clarity and simplicity; he knew that in the very act of condemning certain bad practices of prose writing he was liable to slip into them. If, however, his writing was not always up to his ideal of prose style, it was seldom very far from it. In the first place, he tried really to write his essays, not assemble them from prefabricated phrases. He asked himself questions like these: "What am I trying to say? What words will express it? What image or idiom will make it clearer? Is this image fresh enough to have an effect?"[86] The main consideration was always clarity, and all other considerations yielded to it. Much as Orwell disliked pedantry, he used all of the techniques of the textbook—numbered lists, italics for particularly significant passages, headings in a variety of types, etc., because they made matters clear.

Yet in calling his best prose as clear as a window pane, Orwell did himself an injustice, since the expression suggests that, though his style has the virtue of making facts and ideas transparently clear, it has no character of its own. Actually, Orwell's style is neither a neutral one, nor an imitation of any other writer notable for clarity. Although Orwell in his early years had a great admiration for Maugham's prose and for a brief time may have modeled his own on it, the two styles could not possibly be confused by any reasonably attentive reader. Orwell's prose is, as it were, under a greater pressure than Maugham's is (in the essays that Maugham and Orwell wrote on Dickens this difference is neatly illustrated). At the same time, Orwell's is the more conversational of the two styles, and one reading Orwell's essays keeps thinking of the man behind the writing, not the craftsman; one has the experience that Pascal spoke of with such pleasure, the experience of opening a book expecting to find an author and finding a man. Orwell said that when he read a writer of strong individuality (Swift, Defoe, Stendhal, Flaubert, for instance), he visualized his face somewhere behind the pages. It did not matter whether or not he knew what the writer actually looked like.

> What one sees is the face the writer *ought* to have. Well, in the case of Dickens I see a face that is not quite the face of Dickens's photographs, though it resembles it. . . . It is the face of a man who is always fighting against something, but who fights in the open and is not frightened, the face of a man who is *generously angry*. . . .[87]

A reader with Orwell's habit of visualizing might see such a face behind Orwell's own pages. For he, too, was a man of generous anger, a man who devoted his life to fighting against the evils of his time.

Like his career as an essayist, Orwell's career as a novelist demonstrated his responsibility. Now, none of Orwell's novels approaches greatness, and one or two of them are fairly flat. It is one of the ironies of his life that, although he had been writing first-rate books of essays and political reporting for years, he became widely known for works of fiction; that, indeed, he achieved his greatest fame with *Nineteen Eighty-Four,* his last novel and itself inferior to his first, *Burmese Days.* Orwell was certainly not chasing fame by employing a form more popular than the essay. He did, however, want a wide audience for what he had to say in *Animal Farm* and *Nineteen Eighty-Four*. His sense of responsibility accounts for the forms of both *Animal Farm* and *Nineteen Eighty-Four*; and it also accounts for some of the faults of both books.

The publishing history of Orwell's last two books, together with world history at the time, helps to explain their narrative form and the differences between them. It also shows how Orwell responded to the moral demands upon him as a political writer. Because the British and the Russians were still fighting the Germans, presumably with a common aim, in 1944, Orwell cast *Animal Farm* not in the form of realistic fiction, but in the form of the fable. Even so, four British publishers rejected it on the grounds that it was objectionable to public policy. By the spring of 1945 the Russians were looking less and less like faithful comrades, and Secker and Warburg accepted the book. By the summer of 1945, disillusionment with Russia had increased, and the book sold very well. The American edition appeared in 1946 and was a best seller.

Orwell must have realized while he was writing *Animal Farm* that some people at least would read it as no more than an animal story. He must have realized how close he was running to one of the two special hazards that any writer of fable or fantasy encounters. The first is that of failing to make the narrative and the characters convincing on the concrete level, so that the writing will have only what may be called a puzzle value. In that case its fate will be to attract only those people who are fond of unravelling riddles. The second danger is that of making the work only too convincing on the concrete level. In that case, it will enable readers, editors, and adapters to take the cash and let the credit go. Thus many people read *Gulliver's Travels* in childhood as a fascinating fairy story and never read an unabridged edition of it in their adult lives. Thus *A Connecticut Yankee* becomes for young and old alike merely a comic romp. After the publication of *Animal Farm* it was obvious that Orwell had fallen into the second hazard. A book intended as an attack on totalitarianism had practically been shunted into the children's section.

Another sort of attack was clearly necessary. Orwell was, of course, familiar with the work of the European writers who had published books against totalitarianism. Of these writers he was most interested in Arthur Koestler, and chiefly interested in *Dark-*

ness at Noon. This book, though perhaps Koestler's best work of fiction, is no great novel. Nevertheless, as a piece of propaganda, it has unquestionable advantages over *Animal Farm.* First, whereas Orwell was compelled to speak in the ambiguities of the fable, Koestler could speak unequivocally. Second, although *Darkness at Noon* treats the facts of a political period candidly, it does so in a literary form which has a wider appeal than books of political essays usually have. People who would not read political treatises read the political discussions which alternate with the action of *Darkness at Noon.*

In his essay on Koestler, Orwell comments explicitly on another reason that helps to make *Darkness at Noon* a successful piece of anti-totalitarian propaganda: Koestler had experienced totalitarianism at first hand. In consequence, *Darkness at Noon,* although it does not carry the kind of conviction of truth that a major work of literature does, carries the kind that excellent reporting of personal experience does. It was the lack of any direct experince of totalitarianism, Orwell thought, that makes the bulk of English writing on this theme so dull or slick, so dishonest or naive. There was nothing in English like *Darkness at Noon*

> because there is almost no English writer to whom it has happened to see totalitarianism from the inside.   In Europe, during the past decade and more, things have been happening to middle-class people which in England do not even happen to the working class.   Most of the European writers I mentioned above, and scores of others like them, have been obliged to break the law in order to engage in politics at all; some of them have thrown bombs and fought in street battles, many have been in prison or the concentration camp, or fled across frontiers with false names and forged passports. One cannot imagine, say, Professor Laski indulging in activities of that kind.   England is lacking, therefore, in what one might call concentration-camp literature.[88]

Now, what had happened to "almost no English writer" had, of course, happened to Orwell. He had fought in the Republican trenches and in the streets of Spanish cities; he had been badly wounded; if he had not come as close to being shot by the Communists in a prison yard as Koestler had come to being shot by the Fascists, he had come close enough; certainly he had been forced to flee across the Spanish frontier.

By 1948 the political climate in England permitted once more the publication of direct attacks upon all complexions of totalitarianism: Orwell was free to write the "concentration-camp" novel for which his unusual experiences in Spain had prepared him. Moreover, because of the enormous success of *Animal Farm* his next book was almost certain to be widely read. By 1948, however, Orwell was in worse health than he had ever been before, and in better financial position. With the money that he made from *Animal Farm* he could have simply relaxed for a while. A period of rest might have prolonged his life for many years. Or he could have worked at his leisure on nonpolitical fiction. He recognized the grave limitations that his political emphasis placed upon his novels, and in the last few years of his life he was reading Conrad and planning to write a novel that would explore human relationships, rather than political ones, in the manner that Conrad's novels do. What he actually did was to throw away his chances for a longer life and higher critical esteem, in order to write another anti-totalitarian book.

This last book, *Nineteen Eighty-Four*, is really not a novel at all. It is a combination of tale of terror and political treatise. Some of the deficiencies of *Nineteen Eighty-Four*, however, are due to the necessities of anti-totalitarian propaganda. For instance, there are the excerpts from *The Theory and Practice of Oligarchical Collectivism*, the book supposedly written by Goldstein (to say nothing of the Appendix on Newspeak). The insertion of these pages constitutes more of an interpolation than Aldous Huxley, for instance, who has always been taken to task for this sort of thing, has ever made in any of his novels. If not longer than Huxley's supposed excerpts from diaries, letters, and the like, these extracts are balder. There is not even the pretense that they are anything more than exposition of political history and theory. Such insertions, however, were part of the technique that Koestler had used successfully in *Darkness at Noon*. Besides, there was not time for the proper technique of the novel. Orwell's message (he did not shy away from this word) was more urgent than Koestler's had been; the world would not wait while he transposed his materials wholly into the concrete terms of fiction: such a transformation would have required a whole series of novels (like those of Romains).

The overruling of Orwell's artistic conscience by his political conscience also accounts for another kind of shortcoming in *Nine-*

teen Eighty-Four. The novel describes a society in rather the same way that Aldous Huxley does in *Brave New World,* and with similar results. The description not only crowds the characters out of the novel and interrupts the narrative; it tends to become tedious in itself. Any writer who draws logical conclusions from the given or projects technological lines from the present to the future runs the risk of drawing an excess of conclusions or of projecting a superfluity of lines, the risk of keeping at the intelligent reader long after the point is clear. Even so great a writer as Swift was hard pressed to make some of his points in *Gulliver's Travels* and at the same time avoid tedium. In *Gulliver's Travels* he does not, of course, share exactly the same problem that Huxley and Orwell do in *Brave New World* and *Nineteen Eighty-Four,* but he does have the general problem of the writer who sets up a framework of assumptions for his story and then pursues the implications of his assumptions: how to keep the book from becoming a bore as he fills in more and more details. What can Swift do to keep his scale-drawing from becoming tiresome? One thing he does is to alter the tone from time to time. On one occasion he uses the size of the Lilliputians to convey the pettiness of human beings, but on another he uses it simply for its own sake—as in the scene where Gulliver describes the dresses of the Lilliputian ladies on the green as looking like one English lady's petticoat spread out upon the grass. But by using the Lilliputians at one time to exhibit their doll-like charm and at another to demonstrate the viciousness of human beings, Swift splinters his effects. Similarly, he splinters them when he employs the giants on one occasion to show human ugliness and on another to show nobility of character. In the same way he achieves variety at the expense of unity and consistency by switching point of view. Sometimes he has the reader see human folly through the eyes of Gulliver, but sometimes he has him see it in Gulliver himself.

In *Nineteen Eighty-Four* Orwell's purpose was so urgent that he could not afford to be inconsistent or playful or to change point of view. This is not to suggest that with Swift's greater literary latitude Orwell would have been another Swift. The comparisons that reviewers drew between *Animal Farm* and *Gulliver's Travels* were founded less on the facts than on their enthusiasm. *Animal Farm* is as far from *Gulliver's Travels* as Orwell's political essays are from Swift's pamphlets. Nevertheless, in choosing the form that he did for *Nineteen Eighty-Four,* Orwell put himself at grave disadvantage as an artist. He chose the form because of the advantage it gave him as a propagandist. *Nineteen Eighty-Four* is his last, desperate attack on totalitarianism; his last, desperate warning to democratic socialism. It is a kind of equivalent of the Epilogue of *Crime and Punishment* (which is also clearly open to esthetic criticism, but to which esthetic criticism is, from Dostoevsky's point of view, as irrelevant as musical criticism of shouts of fire would be). Raskolnikov dreams of a plague which is sweeping over the world and causing a vicious madness in all whom it infects. By Orwell's time the dream had become a reality. As Dostoevsky warned Russian intellectuals against what he thought in his time was typically Western, Orwell warned Western intellectuals—and others—against what in our time has become typically Russian.

vi. THE LITERARY CRITICISM

Finally, Orwell's sense of responsibility is demonstrated even in his literary criticism. Orwell was not like the sort of social scientist or historian to whom literature is mere evidence of a trend or a movement. One needs only a slight acquaintance with his literary essays to understand that he read books for their own sakes as well as for the data that they provided. Yet, for the most part, he wrote about books, not for their importance in themselves, but for their importance as historical or personal records, or as symptoms or contributing causes of the state of society in our own time. And because he believed that the importance of subliterature in these respects had been largely ignored, he wrote more about second-rate poetry, boys' magazines, crime novels, and the like than he did about major works of literature.*

The fact that there was a large body of second-rate literature which educated as well as uneducated people were familiar with was itself significant to Orwell. There is, for instance, what one might call a canon of second-rate poetry, the sort of poetry which Orwell, taking a term from Chesterton, describes as "good bad poetry."

> There is a great deal of good bad poetry in English, all of it, I should say, subsequent to 1790. Examples of good bad poems—I am deliberately choosing diverse ones—are "The Bridge of Sighs," "When all the World is Young, Lad," "The Charge of the Light Brigade," Bret Harte's "Dickens in Camp," "The Burial of Sir John Moore," "Jenny Kissed Me," "Keith of Ravelston," "Casabianca." All of these reek of sentimentality, and yet—not these particular poems, perhaps, but poems of this kind, are capable of giving true pleasure to people who can clearly see what is wrong with them. One could fill a fair-sized anthology with good bad poems, if it were not for the significant fact that good bad poetry is usually too well known to be worth reprinting. . . . The fact that such a thing as good bad poetry can exist is a sign of the emotional overlap between the intellectual and the ordinary man. The intellectual *is* different

---

* At the same time, Orwell rather enjoyed subliterature for its own sake. In a way he illustrates himself a remark he makes about professions generally in his essay on Dali: "It seems to be, if not the rule, at least distinctly common for an intellectual bent to be accompanied by a nonrational . . . urge in the same direction. A sculptor, for instance, is interested in planes and curves, but he is also a person who enjoys the physical act of mucking about with clay and stone. An engineer is a person who enjoys the feel of tools, the noise of dynamos and the smell of oil." "Benefit of Clergy: Some Notes on Salvador Dali," *Dickens, Dali and Others*, p. 81.

from the ordinary man, but only in certain sections of his personality, and even then not all the time.[89]

The existence of the canon of second-rate poetry is an encouraging symptom. It indicates to Orwell that unity which is necessary to the progress of democratic socialism. However, works and forms which are more or less popular can also be symptoms of a dangerous sort, symptoms which a man who is concerned with the health of society will watch closely. The contemporary crime novel is such a symptom. Moreover, by comparing the crime novel of today with that of yesterday it is possible to measure, so to speak, the loss of moral health in our time. The crime novel of the nineteenth and early twentieth centuries becomes, if not a symptom of normal good health, a symptom of something very close to it. This, at least, is the implication of "Raffles and Miss Blandish."

Orwell begins "Raffles and Miss Blandish" with an elaborate examination of the most successful story of E. W. Hornung. Raffles is the amateur cracksman, the gentleman crook. The gentlemanly part of Raffles, however, is not just a veneer of personality, but an essential part of the structure of his character. Indeed, by comparison with the heroes of current crime stories Raffles is downright knightly. He is not religious, but he is, in his fashion, scrupulous (it is all right to rob one's fellow guests, but not one's host). Towards women he is not moral, but he is chivalrous. Though no respecter of property, he is intensely patriotic (he joins the Army to fight in the Boer War and dies in combat). He dislikes unnecessary violence and prefers to rob unarmed. The Raffles stories (altogether Hornung wrote four novels in which the amateur cracksman was the hero) have few corpses, little bloodshed, no sex crimes. Though written from the point of view of the criminal, they are, says Orwell, much less "antisocial" than a great many contemporary stories written from the point of view of the detective. "They belong to a time when people had standards, though they happened to be foolish standards. Their key-phrase is 'not done.' "[90]

After his discussion of Raffles Orwell says, "Now for a header into the cesspool,"[91] and begins an analysis of *No Orchids for Miss Blandish,* by James Hadley Chase. He describes in detail the extraordinary violence of the book and then submits: "Affection, friendship, good nature or even ordinary politeness do not enter. . . ."[92] The machinery of the story makes it necessary that Mr. Blandish should want to get his daughter back from the gangsters who have kidnapped her, but this is apparently the only reason for his concern, since the book assumes that the norm of human behavior is complete egoism, if not complete corruption. All of the other people in the novel—police and criminals alike—have only one motive: the pursuit of power; and the only reason that the police are to be preferred to the criminals is that they have more power and use it more efficiently.

The reader of *Raffles* sympathizes with the hero-crook, but he understands that sooner or later Raffles will have to pay for his crimes. But the reader of *No Orchids* understands that one may commit whatever crimes he pleases, so long as he is powerful enough. Whereas the Raffles stories appeal to the normal human desire to be entertained, *No Orchids* appeals to the power instinct. With Raffles the reader escapes from the routine of the ordinary world into a world of rather boyish adventure. With the characters of *No Orchids* he escapes into a world of brutality and perversion. Yet this world, far from being an unreal one, is a reflection of the great world of modern power politics. Most readers of Chase are probably not much interested in politics. In *No Orchids*, however, they have a translation of political struggles into struggles between policemen and racketeers. "People worship power in the form in which they are able to understand it."[93] As Orwell himself said, *No Orchids* is not an entirely new kind of book. Edgar Wallace exhibits some of the same symptoms that Chase does. Wallace's hero is not the free-lance detective who, like Sherlock Holmes, captures criminals by means of his own brilliance and bravery, but the Scotland Yard man who crushes them by means of the powerful organization behind him. And Wallace's policemen are, unlike real English policemen, extremely cruel. Nevertheless, says Orwell, the denial of the distinction between good and evil and the worship of power are comparatively new things in English popular fiction. Although *Raffles* is full of taboos and *No Orchids* forbids nothing, the books are only forty years apart.

Moreover, says Orwell, the cult of power and violence of which *No Orchids* is the epitome is beginning to affect a form of literature even more widely read than the crime novel: the pulp magazine. He is especially disturbed at this indication that the doctrine of "realism," the doctrine that might makes right, is filtering down to the common people.

Orwell, however, was not a mere alarmist, the sort of person who cries destruction and ruin, corruption and doom at the slightest hint of danger, either because he is chronically frightened, or because he has a perverse side which takes a pleasure in the idea of a world corrupted and ruined, or simply because he has got into the habit of crying. Just as his sense of responsibility would not allow him to fail to point out danger, it would not allow him to exaggerate it. In the face of danger he preserved a sense of proportion—like an epidemiologist, who recognizes the gravity of the situation when cases of an infectious disease reach a given number but who does not assume that the population is going to be wiped out in a few weeks.

As a responsible scientist would check one group of data against another, Orwell checks the evidence in the crime novel against the evidence in the penny and twopenny comic postcards that are sold in stationers' shops all over England. In "The Art of Donald McGill" he concludes that though the power-worship and violence, the egoism and corruption of the crime novel have begun to filter down to the common people, they have not filtered very far. At first glance, the world of the comic postcards may seem to be one in which the individual has revolted against all of the restrictions which customs and moral codes have put upon him. Actually, says Orwell, it is a world in which the individual submits to the conventions of a stable and even strict society. For instance, despite the fact that the cards of McGill (apparently both the name of an artist and the trade name of a publishing syndicate employing many artists) are much more obscene than any cartoons that could possibly be published in a magazine or newspaper, they are not intended as pornography; rather they are intended as a parody of it. The voluptuous figures of some of the women do not portray a sexual ideal; they caricature it. The jokes about marriage make no attempt to undermine it; they assume that it is beyond attack. ". . . the jokes about nagging wives and tyrannous mothers-in-law . . . imply a . . . society in which marriage is indissoluble and family loyalty is taken for granted."[94]

The postcards are a safety valve, and what they give vent to is what Orwell calls the Sancho Panza in human beings.

If you look into your own mind, which are you, Don Quixote or Sancho Panza? Almost certainly you are both. There is one part of you that wishes to be a hero or a saint, but another part of you is a little fat man who sees very clearly the advantages of staying alive with a whole skin. . . . His tastes lie toward safety, soft beds, no work, pots of beer and women. . . . He it is who punctures your fine attitudes and urges you to look after Number One, to be unfaithful to your wife, to bilk your debts. . . .[95]

Though the Sancho Panza in the common man's personality to whom the postcards appeal may be a crude and low fellow, at least he is not violent or vicious, like that part of the more sophisticated man's personality to which the paintings of Dali appeal. The common man enjoys such healthy and harmless obscenities as jests about newlyweds and adultery; he does not enjoy such diseased and dangerous obscenities as rotting corpses and dead donkeys with their eyes hacked out. In the popularity of the postcards Orwell sees a symptom of the general good moral health of English society.

Orwell's concern with literature, not as a symptom of the state of society, but as a cause, is exemplified by "Boys' Weeklies." To make an investigation of a form which is not only sub-literary but specifically designed for adolescents would seem to many critics a complete waste of time. What possible importance, they would ask, can this sort of thing have? It is important, Orwell says, because what the boy reads has an effect upon the man. "The worst books are often the most important, because they are usually . . . read earliest in life."[96] The greater part of "Boys' Weeklies" is an examination of two of the oldest and most popular boys' weeklies, *Gem* and *Magnet,* the staple item of which is the school story. From personal experience Orwell learned that the boys who go to the public schools usually read these two magazines but stop reading them at twelve or thereabouts. Boys at cheap private schools, however, continue to read them for another three or four years. Working class boys read them at an even later age (shops in the poor quarters of town almost always stock them). And British legionaries of the French Foreign Legion, Orwell found, were still interested in them.

To discover what kind of effect *Gem* and *Magnet* probably have on their average reader, Orwell examines not only the fiction, but also the advertisements and the correspondence columns. In both the stories and the advertisements, he finds, the glamour of public school life is played up, and the reader is invited to fantasies of nobility and heroics. The letters to the editor show that some of the boys accept the invitation to the extent of living a large part of their lives in a world of fantasy. For instance, one boy gives the editors his height and weight, his chest and biceps measurements, and then asks them to tell him which of the characters in the fourth form at Greyfriars he most closely resembles. One may say, of course, that it is perfectly normal for boys to indulge in outlandish fantasies, and that it is only to be expected that cops-and-robbers literature written for boys in their teens should be absurdly unreal. Orwell, however, is worried about the peculiar kind of unreality of the world of the boys' magazines: it mingles with the ordinary fantasies of boyhood all the popular illusions of the years before World War I. The stories may be set in 1910 or in 1940, he says, but the time makes no difference; the world is always the same.

> You are . . . sitting down to tea in your study . . . after an exciting game of football which was won by an odd goal in the last half-minute. There is a cozy fire in the study and outside the wind is whistling. The ivy clusters thickly round the old grey stones. The King is on his throne and the pound is worth a pound. Over in Europe the comic foreigners are jabbering and gesticulating, but the grim grey battleships of the British Fleet are steaming up the Channel and at the outposts of Empire the monocled Englishmen are holding the natives at bay. After tea we shall sit around the study fire having a good laugh at Billy Bunter and discussing the team for next week's match against Rookwood. Everything is safe, solid and unquestionable. Everything will be the same for ever and ever.[97]

In the latter part of "Boys' Weeklies" Orwell discusses some of the newer magazines (in the five years before he wrote the essay eight new ones had come out). He finds in the new ones the same causes for alarm as in the old ones, and some different causes, too. *Rover, Skipper,* and *Hotspur* are unlike *Gem* and *Magnet* in that violence and bully-worship have become significant motifs. Whereas in the old stories there were a dozen or more boys, all more or less equal in importance, with whom readers of different temperaments could identify themselves, in the new stories there is usually one character who dominates everyone else and "whose usual method

of solving any problem is a sock on the jaw."[98] Yet, as regards
politics and history, the world of the new weeklies is just like that
of the old ones. Nothing has really happened since 1910. There
have been no wars (except as they figure as picturesque back-
grounds) no Nazis or Communists, no concentration camps, no unemployment. The implication of the weeklies is that "the major
problems of our time do not exist, that there is nothing wrong with
laissez-faire capitalism, that foreigners are unimportant comics.
. . ."[99]

Since more than half of the weeklies that Orwell discusses in
his essay are owned by the Amalgamated Press, and so tied closely
to the *Daily Telegraph* and the *Financial Times,* he saw no reason
to believe that the assumptions which run through their pages were
simply the results of the ignorance or laziness of hack writers who
had not got out of the ruts of the early nineteen hundreds. They
were the assumptions which newspaper magnates like Lord Camrose
wished to be made. And he concluded that boys' weeklies were by
no means the least of the reasons why the majority of Englishmen
are patriotic but politically naive, ready to rally to the defense of
England during the times when she is in obvious danger, but
simply not aware of what is going on in the world between these
times, simply not interested.

Orwell's essays on Rudyard Kipling and P. G. Wodehouse are,
respectively, the best examples of his interest in literature as an
historical and as a personal record. Orwell admires Kipling because
Kipling, however wrong he may often have been in his political
and moral attitudes, was never irresponsible.* And Orwell enjoys
a certain amount of Kipling's work (it is "good bad" writing). What
gives Kipling his special value, however, is his record of the British
in India. It is a somewhat tawdry one, but it is the only one we
have. And Orwell is willing to accept the rather uncivilized character of Kipling, since it is part of the unlikely combination of circumstances necessary to produce the record. Civilized men usually

---

* "Kipling sold out to the British governing classes, not financially but emotionally.
This warped his political judgment, for the British ruling classes were not what he
imagined, and it led him into abysses of folly and snobbery, but he gained a corre-
sponding advantage from having at least tried to imagine what action and responsibility are like. It is a great thing in his favor that he is not witty, not 'daring,' has
no wish to *epater les bourgeois.* . . . Even his worst follies seem less shallow and less
irritating than the 'enlightened' utterances of the same period, such as Wilde's
epigrams or the collection of cracker-mottoes at the end of *Man and Superman.*"
"Rudyard Kipling," p. 160.

remain in the centers of civilization, Orwell says, and it is therefore silly to speculate about the novels that George Moore or Thomas Hardy might have written about nineteenth-century Anglo-India. Kipling has recorded

> an immense amount of stuff that one could otherwise only gather from verbal tradition or from unreadable regimental histories. . . . from the body of Kipling's early work there does seem to emerge a vivid and not seriously misleading picture of the old pre-machine gun army—the sweltering barracks in Gibralter or Lucknow, the red coats, the pipeclayed belts and the pillbox hats, the beer, the fights, the floggings, hangings and crucifixions, the bugle calls, the smell of oats and horse-piss, the bellowing sergeants with foot-long mustaches, the bloody skirmishes, invariably mismanaged, the crowded troopships, the cholera-stricken camps, the "native" concubines, the ultimate death in the workhouse. It is a crude, vulgar picture, in which a patriotic music-hall turn seems to have got mixed up with one of Zola's gorier passages, but from it future generations will be able to gather some idea of what a long-term volunteer army was like. On about the same level they will be able to learn something of British India in the days when motor-cars and refrigerators were unheard of.[100]

"In Defense of P. G. Wodehouse" is the sort of title that suggests a chivalrous brief for a minor writer, an argument that his talent, though small, is not contemptible. Orwell had, in fact, read with enjoyment a large portion of the huge output of Wodehouse. And though he would not have said, as some people have, that Wodehouse was a superb comic craftsman who handled English like a poet, he probably would have said that Wodehouse at his best was a "good bad writer." In this essay, however, he is concerned with something which is to him, and presumably to Wodehouse, more important than the question of Wodehouse's position in twentieth-century English fiction. He is concerned with the question of Wodehouse's conduct during World War II.

When the Germans advanced through Belgium in the summer of 1940, they captured Wodehouse, first putting him under house arrest at his villa in Touquet and then putting him in an internment camp. A year later they transferred him to the Adlon Hotel in Berlin and announced that he was going to do some radio broadcasts. Between late June and early July he did five. The first one, however, was not over the German radio. It was an interview with

Harry Flannery of C.B.S. The following, says Orwell are fair specimens of Wodehouse's remarks.

> I never was interested in politics. I'm quite unable to work up any kind of belligerent feeling. Just as I'm about to feel belligerent about some country, I meet a decent sort of chap. We go out together and lose any fighting thoughts or feelings. . . . The only concession I want from Germany is that she gives me a loaf of bread, tells the gentlemen with muskets at the main gate to look the other way, and leaves the rest to me. In return I am prepared to hand over India, an autographed set of my books, and to reveal the secret process of cooking sliced potatoes on a radiator.[101]

The remarks about the lack of belligerence caused great indignation in England. The Germans recorded the interview and rebroadcast it several times. Apparently they interfered very little with the talks Wodehouse delivered over the Nazi radio. The general impression that he gave in these talks, however, was that the Germans had not treated him at all badly and that he had no feelings of enmity. The four talks provoked questions in Parliament, angry editorials, letters of protest from fellow-writers. The *Daily Mirror's* "Cassandra" used expressions such as "selling his country," "Quisling," and "worshipping the Führer." Lending libraries all over England withdrew Wodehouse's books from circulation. The B.B.C. put a ban on his lyrics and kept it on for two years. Three years after the broadcasts, supposedly responsible people were demanding that Wodehouse be tried for treason. Wodehouse had ceased to be funny. He was accused not only of being a traitor who had bought his way out of internment camp, but also of being a Fascist in sympathy. At the time of the talks, letters to the press charged that there were Fascist tendencies in his books. At the time of Orwell's essay, four years afterwards, they were still charging it.

It is this sort of injustice and irresponsibility on the part of people supposedly responsible in a society supposedly just that prompts Orwell to write his essay on Wodehouse. Looked at dispassionately, he says, the broadcasts show that Wodehouse was guilty of nothing more than stupidity, that the motive for making them was simply the comedian's passion for keeping in touch with his audience and getting a laugh. The full texts of the broadcasts, however, were hard to get hold of in 1945. The novels (about a hundred of them altogether, dozens still in print) were not. They are the evidence which Orwell, the advocate rather than the critic, presents in Wodehouse's defense.

Some of Wodehouse's best-known novels, Orwell observes, were written very early in the century; all of his best characters had appeared well before 1925. Although Wodehouse's work may be divided into three periods (the "school," the "American," and the "country house" periods), there is really no development in it. Aside from the fact that there is more money in it, the world of Bertie Wooster is just about the same as the world of Mike Jackson, the schoolboy hero of the early stories. Bertie, invented in 1917, actually reflects the pre-1914 period of English society. By paraphrase and citation from the novels of all three stages of Wodehouse's career, Orwell shows that the picture of the world which Wodehouse had formed in the pre-War years never changed. In none of the novels is there anything but the most superficial awareness of what has happened to England since 1914, to say nothing of what has happened to other countries; in the majority of the novels there is not even that. It was this almost absolute political ignorance, Orwell says, that made it possible for Wodehouse not only to make his broadcasts for the Nazis, but to make them without the slightest suspicion that they would arouse a storm of protests.

Orwell closes his article on Wodehouse by saying that he has tried to show

> how the wretched Wodehouse—just because success and expatriation had allowed him to remain mentally in the Edwardian age—became the *corpus vile* in a propaganda experiment, and I suggest that it is now time to regard the incident as closed.[102]

Obviously, a good deal of work has gone into the Wodehouse essay. The question that might arise among some critics and readers is: was it worth all the trouble? Wodehouse had been slandered and unjustly suppressed (always assuming that Orwell's case is a sound one). But the ban on his lyrics had been lifted by the time of Orwell's essay. The libraries were probably beginning to circulate his books again. The demands that he be indicted for treason were tapering off. In fact, it was a pretty safe bet that in a few more years the whole affair would be forgotten (as, apparently, it has been; at least it has been forgiven: Herbert Jenkins is even bringing out a uniform edition of the complete works of Wodehouse).

And Wodehouse is, after all (the argument might go on), just a comedian who got himself into the fix that some other popular entertainers did by singing or dancing for the Nazis. Yet here is Orwell defending this literary nobody when he could be writing an essay on Joyce or Eliot. Then consider the essays that have preceded this last one on Wodehouse in a book called *Critical Essays* in Great Britain. There are only two on clearly major figures, those on Dickens and Yeats, and the second is very short. Next in order of importance are the pieces on Kipling and Wells. After that we come down to one on a journalistic novelist, Arthur Koestler. Besides these, there are essays on the writing and painting of Dali, the crime novel, boys' weeklies, and comic postcards. Admitting that in *Shooting an Elephant* Orwell has an essay on Tolstoy and Shakespeare and another one on Swift, let us also notice that there are also essays on "good bad books," nonsense poetry, and *Helen's Babies*. Nowhere in the three volumes of criticism in which Orwell's literary essays are collected is there an essay on Eliot (there are only scattered remarks) or Faulkner, Gide or Mann.

The answer to all this is that, first of all, Orwell did not, in the main, ignore the greatest writers and concentrate on the smaller ones out of mere perversity or mere ignorance. He was no British equivalent of Gilbert Seldes, saying that the comic postcard is a greater art form than the novel, or that the verse of Edward Lear is more important than the poetry of T. S. Eliot. Such inversions would probably have seemed to him merely a new way of being precious—by being vulgar. However scornfully or impatiently Orwell may have swept aside the usual assumptions of conventional critical theory, his judgment of the stature of any given writer agrees with accepted critical opinion more often than it disagrees. The main reason that he devoted so much of his energy to the examination of subliterature was that he believed that it was more closely connected than major literature sometimes was with certain forces in our time which responsible men must watch. The greater part of his criticism, then, is prompted by Orwell's recognition of the responsibility which the writer, like any other man, owes to society. The essay on Wodehouse, however, is prompted by his recognition of the responsibility which society owes the individual. Orwell ignored many a great name in literature, and he rejected an important critical question: whether the laurels are on the right brows. He attended, however, in his criticism as much as in the rest of his writing, to another important question: whether the nooses are around the wrong necks.

CHAPTER 2

Perspective on Power

i. THE EXAMINATION OF POWER

LIKE his attitude toward authority, Orwell's attitude toward power was a paradoxical balance: a great revulsion and an equally great resolution. He could detect the presence of power and the desire for it in minimal amounts and under camouflages that would conceal them from most people (for instance under the pacifism and sanctity of Tolstoy). Yet he was not intimidated by the greatest concentrations, the greatest displays of power. He was horrified by the evils of power, not terrified.

In the last stage of his career Orwell was preoccupied by the evils of totalitarian power. In the first he was preoccupied by the evils of imperialistic power. His main attack on imperialism is his first novel, *Burmese Days.*

According to the official view at the time, the British rule in Burma was enlightened and benevolent. According to Orwell's view, it was the reverse. Provincial and philistine, the British were indifferent to Burmese culture or contemptuous of it. More barbarous than the people whom they ruled, they regarded the Burmese as a lower order of creatures, to be treated like domestic animals when they were tractable and like wild ones when they were not. No Englishman who could not enjoy, or at least acquiesce in, the exploitation of a conquered country, the inflicting of injustice and suffering on native soldiers and servants, the degradation of the few professional men among a subject people, and—in one way or another—the self-aggrandizement that the strong can get at the expense of the weak, could last long in Orwell's Burma. Neither could any English woman, and the English wives in

Burmese Days are (like some in *A Passage to India*) on occasion more power-hungry, even more blood-thirsty than the men.

All of these generalizations are made concrete in the short, unhappy life of Flory, the hero of *Burmese Days*. Flory takes up his duties in Burma to find that he is surrounded by colonels who argue that "these bloody nationalists should be boiled in oil," merchants who refer to all Orientals as "greasy little babus,"[1] and whippersnappers just out of school who kick grey-haired Burmese butlers. In this society Flory becomes a heretic because he regards the native population as human, takes an interest in Burmese arts, and even has an Indian for a close friend. The continual conflict between Flory's heresy and the orthodoxy of the British colony reaches a new height when an order arrives that, for the sake of appearances, a native or two should be nominated for membership in British clubs. The question at Flory's station is whether he will dare to nominate his Indian doctor friend.

Flory believes that an English girl who has just come to the station (ostensibly to visit an aunt and uncle, actually to find a husband) will help him to choose the difficult but honorable course of proposing the doctor for the club. For a long while he has wished for someone who would share his values, and Elizabeth seems such a woman. However, he and Elizabeth have their first moment of rapport when they shoot some of the green pigeons (birds so beautiful that Flory feels a pang when he looks up at them) which Orwell has earlier used as a symbol for Flory's values and his view of Burma. Elizabeth can respond to beauty only by destroying it, although—in a reversal of Wilde's maxim—she loves the thing she kills: after she has shot the pigeon, she puts it to her breast and caresses it. She also wants to kiss Flory, who has also killed.

But a rival shows up at the station, an aggressively virile cavalry lieutenant. Elizabeth is captivated by Verral, who takes no nonsense from natives or horses. His mastery over animals, something of which he teaches to Elizabeth, does almost as much to make her succumb to him as the power which he exerts directly upon her. He easily seduces her and then leaves without even saying goodbye. Elizabeth would now be willing to settle for Flory as a second-best suitor, except for one thing. Flory's political opponents bribe the Burmese girl who was formerly Flory's mistress to make a dreadful scene in public. It is not, however, Flory's having kept a Burmese girl that turns Elizabeth completely against him. "He might have committed a thousand abominations and she would have forgiven him. But not after that shameful, squalid scene, and the devilish ugliness of his disfigured face [Flory has a birthmark] in that moment."[2] Like Verral, like the typical Englishman at the station, Elizabeth lacks compassion for the weak, the unfortunate, the handicapped, the ugly. She has, as Forster said of the British in India, an undeveloped heart, and Burma belongs to those with undeveloped hearts. At the end of the book Flory commits suicide; Elizabeth marries the deputy commissioner. "Her servants live in constant terror of her. . . . She . . . knows how to put the wives of subordinate officials in their places—in short, she fills with complete success the position . . . of a burra memsahib."[3]

With its criticism of the Empire and its investigation of the culture of a subject people, *Burmese Days* virtually demands comparison with *A Passage to India*. The results are not in Orwell's favor (and it would be unreasonable to expect Orwell's first novel to equal Forster's last). Forster's style, imaginative and resonant, shows up the defects of Orwell's. V. S. Pritchett has called Orwell's writing "flat." Actually, it is not at all flat in the usual sense, because, in the first place, Orwell thought with his own head and, in the second place, he had a passion for purity and exactness of language. Admirably clear and clean, it is from the beginning an ideal style for exposition, but in *Burmese Days* it is still a bit bare for the novel.

More important, Orwell's insights are inferior to Forester's. Though he thought with his own head, in *Burmese Days* his head was not as cool as it later became. The book is written too soon after the events by a man too closely involved in them. If his job as policeman made Orwell hate the Empire, it also made him hate the Burmese almost as much. Though victims of tyranny, they were sometimes intolerably impudent victims. Then, as later, Orwell would undoubtedly have been willing to die for justice, but he found it hard to be charitable. Forster sees something sympathetic about most of the people, both Indian and British, in *A Passage to India* at the same time that he perceives their shortcomings and even their vices. Orwell can scarcely do better than despise one character in *Burmese Days* a little less than another. Of course, a novelist need not like any of his characters, but he is obliged (as Graham Greene has said) to give them their due. In *Burmese Days* Orwell failed this obligation.

A few years later Orwell was able to look at British imperialism more objectively. He then saw that, bad as it was, the form of power with which he had dealt in *Burmese Days* was not chemically pure. The Blimps who administered the Empire had no overall theory of imperialism and, although they had undeveloped hearts, they did not have absolutely selfish or absolutely ruthless ones. Their very provinciality was a species of patriotism. If they had a rough notion of justice for subject peoples, at least they were not without scruples. Even their widely criticized hypocrisy had its good side: since they kept telling themselves that they were ruling the natives for their own good, they could not be as brutal as they otherwise could have been. Crossed up by contradictions and confusions, their exercise of power was not only unsystematic, but sometimes downright clumsy. And through a few men like Flory, even kindness kept creeping in.

The totalitarian rulers of the twentieth century suffer no such mental or moral confusion; rather they suffer from what is almost a monomania: about the only thing that really interests them is power. They are not hobbled in their quest for power by any notions of even rough justice for their subjects; they have thrown off the weight of conscience that the imperialist carried when he took up the white man's burden. Of course, this truth is not admitted in anything spoken or written for public consumption. Instead, there is a great deal of mealy-mouthed talk about the benevolence of the government, about the personal sacrifices its officials make and the pains they undergo for the good of their people. In *Nineteen Eighty-Four* Orwell sums up all this show of benevolence in the pictures of Big Brother which are plastered on the walls of half the buildings in Oceania. He sums up the truth behind Big Brother's smile in one of the scenes where Winston is tortured, interrogated, and instructed by O'Brien. In the course of the ghastly catechism which he is teaching Winston, O'Brien asks him why the Party clings to power. Winston supposes that O'Brien wants him to say that the Party desires power not for its own ends, but for the good of the masses, who, because they are weak and cowardly, need to be ruled by men who are strong and

brave. Therefore he answers, "You are ruling over
good." At this, O'Brien turns high the dial of the
inflicts pain on Winston when he gives incorrect
he gives Winston the correct answer:

> The Party seeks power entirely for its own sake. We are not
> interested in the good of others; we are interested solely in power.
> . . . We are different from all the oligarchies of the past in that
> we know what we are doing. All the others . . . were cowards and
> hypocrites. . . . They pretended, perhaps they even believed, that
> they had seized power unwillingly and for a limited time, and that
> just around the corner there lay a paradise where human beings
> would be free and equal. . . . We know that no one ever seizes
> power with the intention of relinquishing it. Power is not a
> means; it is an end.[4]

The violence by which power is acquired and maintained is
another aspect of totalitarianism that Orwell stresses in *Nineteen
Eighty-Four*. The violence of O'Brien's pedagogy is preceded by
that of Winston's arrest, his detention, and his preliminary inter-
rogation. Winston and Julia are enjoying an evening in their
room above the second-hand shop when suddenly a ladder is
thrust through the window. In a few moments the place is full
of policemen stamping about in iron-shod boots and flourishing
rubber truncheons. Winston and Julia are ordered into the middle
of the room and stand there trembling with understandable appre-
hension.

> There was a gasp and a thump behind him, and he received a
> violent kick on the ankle which nearly flung him off his balance.
> One of the men had smashed his fist into Julia's solar plexus,
> doubling her up like a pocket ruler. She was thrashing about on
> the floor, fighting for breath.[5]

In the common cell in which he is first held, Winston watches
scenes which are horribly brutal but obviously routine, of which
this is one:

> He [the guard] took his stand opposite the chinless man, and then,
> at a signal from the officer, let free a frightful blow, with all the
> weight of his body behind it, full in the chinless man's mouth. The
> force of it seemed almost to knock him clear of the floor. His body
> was flung across the cell. . . . Amid a stream of blood and saliva,
> the two halves of a dental plate fell out of his mouth.[6]

Then it is Winston's turn.

> How many times he had been beaten, how long the beatings had con-
> tinued, he could not remember. Always there were five or six
> men in black uniforms at him simultaneously. Sometimes it was
> fists, sometimes it was truncheons, sometimes it was steel rods,
> sometimes it was boots.[7]

The violence is not confined to the prisons of Oceania; it is
part and parcel of the whole life of the state. Police with truncheons and machine guns patrol the streets. Barbed wire is stretched
across intersections as though they were battlefields. Besides ruling
their people by violence, the Inner Party encourages them in, and
in fact compels them to, experiences of vicarious violence. They
must watch newsreels of enemy civilians being machinegunned
and attend public hangings of war prisoners. Every morning there
is a "Two Minutes' Hate," during which television programs are
used to stimulate everyone into fiercely aggressive feelings against
Goldstein, the Trotsky figure of Oceania and the supposed leader
of the underground. Once a year the aggressive feelings are kept
at their height for a solid "Hate Week," the preparations for
which take hundreds of hours of the citizens' time.

In any ordinary week of the year the citizens of Oceania spend
most of their time after working hours in state projects or drives
of one kind or another, which are only nominally voluntary. This
lack of private life is yet another characteristic that Orwell em-
phasizes in *Nineteen Eighty-Four*. Even during the few hours
that he is allowed at home the citizen does not escape from the
state. Police patrols in helicopters skim between buildings and
peer into windows. In every room there is a television set which
can transmit as well as receive, and no one can tell when the police
are plugged into his. "You had to live—did live, from habit that
became instinct—in the assumption that every sound you made
was overheard and, except in darkness, every movement scruti-
nized."[8]

Still, Julia tells Winston before they are arrested, there is a
limit to the Party's invasion of the individual's privacy. "They
can't get inside you," she says, and Winston sees at least a minimal
hope in her remark.

> They could spy upon you night and day, but if you kept your
> head you could still outwit them. With all their cleverness they had

never mastered the secret of finding out what another human being was thinking. Perhaps that was less true when you were actually in their hands. One did not know what happened inside the Ministry of Love, but it was possible to guess: tortures, drugs . . . persistent questionings. Facts . . . could be squeezed out of you by torture. But if the object was not to stay alive but to stay human, what difference did it ultimately make? They could not alter your feelings. . . . They could lay bare in the utmost detail everything that you had done or said or thought; but the inner heart, whose workings were mysterious even to yourself, remained impregnable.[9]

During their imprisonment, however, Winston and Julia learn that, whenever it wishes to, the Party can invade the privacy of the inmost mind and heart. Even before O'Brien is finished with him, Winston has no mind of his own. The Party has contrived means to drain the ideas out of it and fill it with theirs. Earlier Winston has written in his diary that freedom is the freedom to say that two and two make four. Now he has lost the ability not only to say that two and two make four, but even to believe it if O'Brien says that they make three or five. When O'Brien has finally finished with him, Winston has lost even his heart to the Party. He and Julia meet after their release, but the only feeling they have for each other is a dull contempt and dislike.

"I betrayed you," she said baldly.

"I betrayed you," he said.

She gave him another quick look of dislike.

"Sometimes," she said, "they threaten you with something—something you can't stand up to, can't even think about. And then you say, 'Don't do it to me, do it to somebody else, do it to so-and-so.' And perhaps you might pretend, afterwards, that it was only a trick and that you just said it to make them stop and didn't really mean it. But that isn't true. . . . You *want* it to happen to the other person. . . . All you care about is yourself."

"All you care about is yourself," he echoed.

"And after that, you don't feel the same toward the other person any longer."[10]

In the early stages of Winston's processing, O'Brien relies on the customary brutalities of beatings, lack of sleep, and starvation to extract from Winston confessions of treason and other crimes. In the later stages he resorts to powerful and subtle scientific instruments and techniques. Yet the Party, though it uses science to maintain and extend its power, officially denies the fundamental scientific assumption of an objective world which is governed by order and in the invesigation of which trained men can confirm one another. The official philosophy of Oceania accords with the observation that Orwell made in "Looking Back on the Spanish War." "Nazi theory . . . specifically denies that such a thing as 'the truth' exists. There is . . . no such thing as 'Science.' There is only 'German Science,' 'Jewish Science,' etc."*

The paragraph from which this sentence is taken deals primarily with history and continues: "The implied objective of this line of thought is a nightmare world in which the Leader, or some ruling clique, controls not only the future but *the past.* If the Leader says of such and such an event, 'It never happened' —well, it never happened."[11] When Orwell wrote this, in 1943, the totalitarian world had already made more than a little progress toward the nightmare world. Orwell once remarked to Arthur Koestler that history had stopped in 1936, and Koestler instantly understood what he meant. The allusion was, of course, to the Spanish Civil War, but both men, Orwell says, were also thinking of totalitarianism in general. In *Darkness at Noon* (1941) Koestler deals with the totalitarian treatment of history:

> Not only the portraits on the walls, but also the shelves in the legation library were thinned out. The disappearance of certain books and brochures happened discreetly, usually the day after the arrival of a message from above. . . .
>
> New books arrived, too; the classics of social science appeared with new footnotes and commentaries, the old histories were replaced by new histories, the old memoirs of dead revolutionary leaders were replaced by new memoirs of the same defunct. Rubashov remarked jokingly to Arlova that the only thing left to be done was to publish a new and revised edition of the back numbers of all newspapers.[12]

Orwell deals with the totalitarian approach to history by turning the joke into grim fact. Winston and his colleagues in the Records Department of the Ministry of Truth spend their days (and many

---

* In *Nineteen Eighty-Four* the applications of science are confined to instruments of torture and instruments of war. The Party does not exploit the possibilities of science for increasing the wealth and comfort of Oceania, because people are easier to govern when they are poor and miserable.

of their nights) revising newspaper stories, speeches, statistics, etc. When all the necessary corrections in a particular number of a newspaper are assembled, it is reprinted, the old copy is destroyed, and the new one is filed in its stead.

In one of the sections of *Nineteen Eighty-Four* purporting to come from Goldstein's *The Theory and Practice of Oligarchical Collectivism* Orwell italicizes the totalitarian revision of human memories.

> . . . it is also necessary to *remember* that events happened in the desired manner. And if it is necessary to rearrange one's memories or to tamper with written records, then it is necessary to *forget* that one has done so. The trick of doing this can be learned like any other mental technique. It *is* learned by the majority of Party members, and certainly by all who are intelligent as well as orthodox. In Oldspeak it is called, quite frankly, "reality control." In Newspeak it is called doublethink. . . .[13]

Newspeak is the official language of Oceania. It is constructed upon observations which Orwell had made earlier in his essays, and it shows how even language becomes a means of maintaining power in a totalitarian state. In *Nineteen Eighty-Four* Winston's friend Syme is employed on the eleventh edition of the Newspeak Dictionary, the purpose of which is to produce a more efficient version of the official language. Well before the composition of *Nineteen Eighty-Four,* however, totalitarian countries had produced what were, in effect, workable versions of Newspeak. The tenth edition of the dictionary was, so to speak, in use at the time Orwell wrote *Nineteen Eighty-Four.* "Even in the early decades of the twentieth century," Orwell writes in the Appendix to *Nineteen Eighty-Four* called "The Principles of Newspeak,"

> telescoped words and phrases had been one of the characteristic features of political language, and it had been noticed that the tendency to use abbreviations of this kind was most marked in totalitarian countries. Examples were such words as Nazi, Gestapo, Comintern. . . .[14]

Syme's job is not only to telescope words and phrases, but to eliminate them. Eventually the Party will have narrowed the range of thought to such an extreme that the very thinking of unorthodox thoughts will be impossible.

Provided the citizen of the totalitarian state has no rebellious instincts at the start, the discipline of totalitarian linguistics can do (up to a point) by non-violent means what the instruments of the torture chamber do by violent ones. In "Politics and the English Language" Orwell indicates the robot-like results of the discipline:

> . . . one often has the curious feeling that one is not watching a live human being but some kind of dummy: a feeling which suddenly becomes stronger at moments when the light catches the speaker's spectacles and turns them into blank discs which seem to have no eyes behind them. And this is not altogether fanciful. A speaker who uses that kind of phraseology has gone some distance toward turning himself into a machine. The appropriate noises are coming out of his larynx, but his brain is not involved. . . .[15]

The self-plagiarism, conscious or unconscious, of the above in the following passage from *Nineteen Eighty-Four* indicates the stress that Orwell put on this feature of totalitarianism. Winston is sitting at a table in the canteen, talking to Syme but giving part of his attention to a man at another table.

> His head was thrown back a little, and because of the angle at which he was sitting, his spectacles caught the light and presented to Winston two blank discs instead of eyes. . . . Just once Winston caught a phrase —"complete and final elimination of Goldstein" —jerked out very rapidly and, as it seemed, all in one piece, like a line of type cast solid. For the rest, it was just a noise, a quack-quack-quacking. . . . Whatever it was, you could be certain that every word was pure orthodoxy. As he watched the eyeless face with the jaw moving rapidly up and down, Winston had a curious feeling that this was not a real human being but some kind of dummy. It was not the man's brain that was speaking; it was his larynx.[16]

ii. THE REJECTION OF PROPHECY

The inordinate desire for power, and the violence, abolition of private life, and manipulation of the truth to serve that desire which Orwell describes in *Nineteen Eighty-Four* indicate clearly enough that Orwell regarded totalitarianism with horror. It is just as great a mistake, however, to read the novel as a prediction of universal totalitarianism before the turn of the century as it is to read it as a mere "psychological necessity" of Orwell's temperament. Nevertheless, critics and common readers alike have taken *Nineteen Eighty-Four* to be an essay in political prediction. Wyndham Lewis, for instance, calls it a "prophetic Wellsian nightmare of events in the future" and a "menacing blueprint of a horrible world only thirty years hence."[17]

Now in the first place, it would be strange if Orwell had offered *Nineteen Eighty-Four* as political prediction, since he had always looked upon that branch of writing with suspicion. "Political predictions are usually wrong, because they are usually based on wish-thinking. . . ."[18] H. G. Wells, for instance, liked to think of history as a process by which the madness in the world represented by the witch-doctor, the war-lord, and the demagogue was driven out by the sanity represented by the scientist. And so he refused to see any great danger in Hitler and predicted a quick end to his career. "Hitler," says Orwell, "is all the war-lords and witch-doctors in history rolled into one. Therefore, argues Wells, he is an absurdity, a ghost from the past, a creature doomed to disappear almost immediately."[19]

Others, who were impressed not by science, but by power, predicted for Hitler conquests no less sweeping than he predicted for himself; but as soon as he suffered a setback or two, they put the Russians in as candidates for world conquest. It is a characteristic of those who worship power, Orwell said, to assume that the direction in which events are moving at any given time is the direction in which they will continue to move. "If the Japanese have conquered South Asia, then they will keep South Asia for ever; if the Germans have captured Tobruk, they will infallibly capture Cairo; if the Russians are in Berlin, it will not be long before they are in London: and so on."[20]

Another of Orwell's objections to political predictors was that they expected things to happen too quickly and completely in areas that stretch beyond battlefields. "The slowness of historical change, the fact that any epoch always contains a great deal of the last epoch, is never sufficiently allowed for."[21]

If Orwell had submitted *Nineteen Eighty-Four* as a prediction, therefore, he would have taken the actual tempo of political and social change into account. Actually, he makes no pretense of taking it into account. England is merely part of one of three huge super-states. All sense of English nationality has disappeared.* Even supposing that the totalitarian methods of rewriting history could be perfected and refined so that no trustworthy written records of the past could be found, there would still remain the whole body of tradition that comes down by word of mouth. Yet Winston cannot even find anyone who remembers a nursery rhyme from beginning to end until the officer of the secret police who traps him quotes an appropriately violent sample.

But the secret policeman, thoroughly indoctrinated, breathing the Party atmosphere like the air itself—in short, Koestler's man without an umbilical cord—is not a likely source of any such quotation. The likely source is one of the common people, the "proles," who (because they presumably do not constitute a threat to the Party) are not disciplined and indoctrinated. When, however, Winston tries to find out what life in England was like before his time by talking to one of the "proles," he learns nothing at all. The mind of the man to whom he talks is not a record, but a rubbish heap of senile irrelevancies. Orwell's purpose is not to show the reader a plausible picture of society "thirty years hence" (thousands of men would have memories more pertinent than that of the man Winston talks to); his purpose is to bring to sharp focus, through the frustration of Winston, the plight of people whose links with their national traditions are being cut right now.

Nor is there any pretense to the plausible in Orwell's picture of the science and technology of the future. If he attributes to Oceania social changes that would be impossible in a generation, he neglects scientific advances that would be perfectly possible. Even if he had wished to, he could not have worked out the details of another *Brave New World,* since he lacked Aldous Huxley's

---

* Orwell deliberately disregards the fact that totalitarianism takes different forms in different countries because of differences in culture, and the fact (which he pointed out in his essays) that all the impulses of the English are against being "coordinated."

extensive knowledge of the various branches of science.* Actually, he had no desire to do so. What chiefly struck him about the modern world was not that men have invented new machinery to break up the bodies and minds of men, but that some men should not hesitate to use it on others. The horror is not in the new means, but in the willingness to use any means, ancient or modern, to the ends of power. What finally forces Winston to betray Julia is the threat of being attacked by rats, a strategem not from our time but from Imperial China.

Far from being a picture of the totalitarianism of the future, *Nineteen Eighty-Four* is, in countless details, a realistic picture of the totalitarianism of the present. For instance, there is nothing novel in damming up the sexual instincts and canalizing them into political directions—into leader-worship, hatred, and war hysteria. Neither is there anything original in distorting the normal feelings of the family to political ends, so that the child becomes an extension of the secret police, spying on his frightened parents day and night. As for the police themselves, their constant surveillance of the citizens, their sudden knocking on the victim's door in the middle of the night, his disappearance without any regard for due process—all this is recognizable even to people who during the past twenty-five years have got their political education from the movies. The inquisitorial routine, the faked confessions, and the trumped-up court proceedings have been common knowledge ever since the reports of the Moscow Trials. And so with the arrangements in concentration camps, where political prisoners are put in charge of the lowest types of criminals and given the worst and dirtiest jobs. So with the abrupt switching of the enemy, the laws so ill-defined that any man can be charged with any crime, the doctrine that the end justifies the means, the five-year plans, the claim to have invented everything.

From the middle thirties until his death Orwell was a propagandist harping on the significance of totalitarianism because he knew that thousands upon thousands of people in democratic countries were only remotely aware of it, and still more thousands thought that there was a lot to be said for it in one form or another. *Nineteen Eighty-Four* is his fiercest piece of propaganda.

---

* But he had a shrewd understanding of its roots. He knew that the empiricism of science is the enemy of all such nonsense as the "biology" of the Nazis, the "ethics" of the Communists, and the "metaphysics" of Oceania.

In it he imposes totalitarianism, with all its horrors, on England in order to make the reader do what he said in his essay on Arthur Koestler was so difficult for an Englishman to do: imagine himself the victim of totalitarianism.

Nineteen Eighty-Four, then, is not a prediction, but an alert. It no more indicates that universal totalitarianism is inevitable than a danger sign on a highway indicates that a wreck is. Orwell frequently criticized other writers for attributing too much in history to inexorable process and too little to human will; a recurring phrase in his essays is that such and such a political, social, or economic development is looked upon "as though it were a law of nature." He believed that there were some directions in which the future could not develop, but not that it could develop in only one direction.

Orwell's interest in nature shows, moreover, that he had some confidence in the direction that the future would take. Talking of the tree that is said to have been planted by the Vicar of Bray leads him to talk of the trees that he has planted himself:

> Even an apple tree is liable to live for about 100 years, so that the Cox I planted in 1936 may be bearing fruit well into the twenty-first century. An oak or beech may live for hundreds of years and be a pleasure to thousands or tens of thousands of people before it is finally sawn up into timber. I am not suggesting that one can discharge all one's obligations toward society by means of a private reafforestation scheme. Still, it might not be a bad idea, every time you commit an anti-social act, to make a note of it in your diary, and then, at the appropriate season, push an acorn into the ground.[22]

Earlier in the essay Orwell says, "A thing which I regret, and which I will try to remedy sometime, is that I have never in my life planted a walnut."[23] A man who concerns himself with planting trees in the forties is not expecting the civilized world to come to an end in the eighties.

CHAPTER 3

Socialism and Nostalgia

i. THE NECESSITY OF SOCIALISM

LIKE his attitudes toward authority and power, Orwell's attitude towards socialism was paradoxical. From at least 1936 on, he was in the advance guard of the crusaders for socialism, yet he moved with some reluctance to his objective and looked back regretfully at much of what the march to socialism necessarily leaves behind. For instance, he was as firmly convinced as any orthodox socialist that, as long as capitalism continued, the working man would be half-starved some of the time and brow-beaten most of the time, and that the lower middle classes would be neglected, discriminated against, and exploited. Still he dreaded government paternalism almost as much as any reactionary and deplored the fact that, for the good of the average citizen, a socialistic government would have to invade certain areas of life in which under capitalism, with all its faults, the common man was free to do as he pleased. Ardently as he desired the better standard of living which socialism would bring to the British working man, he would have had a wry appreciation of the joke which defines socialism as a system under which people will damned well eat strawberries and cream whether they like them or not. By a similar ambivalence, his scorn for the aristocrat was matched by his disgust for most of his fellow socialists. Aristocrats were museum pieces at best and parasites at worst, but socialists were likely to be eccentrics who wanted to impose their peculiar tastes and way of life on everyone else. Again, although Orwell knew perfectly well that a socialistic society implied a highly mechanized society, he had a strong aversion to twentieth-century machinery and to both the specific goods and the cultural atmosphere that it produced. He was aware that a socialistic state would have to be run in the most efficient way that modern technology could provide, but personally he found it more attractive to do some things the hard way: he preferred coal fires to central heating and candles to electric light.

Of all the evils that proclaimed to Orwell the need for a socialistic England, none was greater than the straightened circumstances in which thousands upon thousands of English working families lived during good times and the squalor in which they lived during bad ones. To see how much socialism he wanted, Orwell said, he had to see for himself exactly how bad the working man's life could be under capitalism. And so he got a commission from Victor Gollancz to investigate conditions in the North of England and Wales, where the depression of the thirties was at its worst, and to write a book (*The Road to Wigan Pier*).

If his investigation were to be worthwhile, he thought, he would have to get to know some of the workers intimately. Getting acquainted with working men turned out to be more difficult than getting acquainted with tramps. Anyone can go tramping, but how do you get a job as a miner or a bricklayer? And who would want to take a job from a real worker? If, however, you cannot work with the miner or the bricklayer, you can live with him. Orwell stayed at both private homes and boarding houses, eating the same food that the poor ate, sleeping in their crowded bedrooms, washing in their primitive and makeshift way.

What did Orwell learn about the shortcomings of capitalism and the consequent need for socialism by living with working-class families that he could not have learned by frequenting liberal drawing rooms and public meetings, by reading government statistics of unemployment and surveys by social workers? First of all, he unlearned what might be called the folklore of liberalism. For instance, he found that the average working-class boy does not feel cheated because he is taken out of school to do a job. On the contrary, he yearns for the day when he will leave school and begin to do "real work." Orwell also learned that the worst sort of landlord is not a fat capitalist living out of sight and odor of the slums, but a poor widow who has put her meager savings into a couple of old houses, lives in one and rents the other and has no money for repairs.

Yet after the sentimentalities and the stereotypes have been disposed of, the truth is still more terrible than anyone is likely to imagine it, and socialism is more urgent than even the most zealous of theoretical socialists realize.

First there are the physical conditions of the slums. Orwell's notebooks are full of descriptions of overcrowding and dirt. The following passage is a sort of summing up.

> Quite often you have eight or even ten people living in a three-roomed house. One of those rooms is a living-room, and as it measures probably a dozen feet square and contains, besides the kitchen range and the sink, a table, some chairs, and a dresser, there is no room in it for a bed. So there are eight or ten people sleeping in two small rooms, probably in at most four beds. . . . Then there is the misery of leaking roofs and oozing walls, which in winter makes some rooms almost uninhabitable. Then there are the bugs. . . . And there are the special miseries attendant upon back-to-back houses. A fifty yards' walk to the lavatory or the dust-bin is not exactly an inducement to be clean. . . . To begin with, the smell, the dominant and essential thing, is indescribable. But the squalor and confusion! A tub of filthy water here, a basin of unwashed crocks there. . . .[1]

By seeing poverty from the inside Orwell learned that the psychological conditions under which the poor live cry out for socialism no less than the physical conditions do. The poor have not, as callous and complacent people think or pretend to think, adapted themselves to their environment. They are not indifferent to dirt, to ugliness, to drudgery. When, from his railway compartment, Orwell observes a girl in a Northern slum, he sees more than meets the eye of the average person who, however sympathetically, sees the poor from the outside only.

> At the back of one of the houses a young woman was kneeling on the stones, poking a stick up the leaden waste-pipe which ran from the sink inside and which I suppose was blocked. . . . She looked up as the train passed, and I was almost near enough to catch her eye. She had a round pale face, the usual exhausted face of the slum girl who is twenty-five and looks forty, thanks to miscarriages and drudgery; and it wore . . . the most desolate, hopeless expression I have ever seen. . . . She knew well enough what was happening to her—understood as well as I did how dreadful a destiny

it was to be kneeling there in the bitter cold, on the slimy stones of a slum backyard, poking a stick up a foul drain-pipe.[2]

The psychological effects of unemployment among the working classes were much worse, Orwell discovered, than they were among the tramps. A tramp may carry all of his possessions in a small bundle, but his mental and moral burdens are lighter than those of the unemployed man who is not on the road but home with his family. The tramp has no roof over his head, but neither does he have to worry about the rent. If he does not have the satisfactions of a wife and children, he does not suffer any remorse for failing to provide for them. He is a man of no expectations and no responsibilities. Terrible as his destitution is, it is not so terrible as "respectable" poverty. Orwell was shocked to find that men who, after perhaps a lifetime of employment, were out of work blamed themselves for not having jobs. When millions of men are out of work, it is part of the economic nature of things for Bert Jones to be out of a job. But Alf Smith is working, and so Jones feels dishonored and a failure. "Hence that frightful feeling of impotence and despair which is almost the worst evil of unemployment."[3]

Capitalism could not bring remedies, not even superficial ones, to the economic ills of the working classes without adding to their spiritual ills. The dole enabled working men to keep alive, but upper-class talk about the lazy, idle men on the dole percolated down to the working classes and made them feel guiltier than ever. One reason that the working classes did not go completely to pieces spiritually on the dole (Orwell said) was that they ultimately recognized that they were not to blame for their ills, that they recognized that there was something fundamentally wrong with capitalism. Another reason was that they improvised a kind of socialism of their own. To unify the unemployed, to prevent them from scabbing during strikes, and to provide them with legal advice when they got tied up in the red tape of relief procedures, a group of men just as ill-clothed and ill-fed as the rest of the jobless population organized a successful National Unemployed Workers' Movement. Yet another reason why the working classes did not lose heart entirely was that they had the instinctive good sense to turn to cheap luxuries to compensate for their misery and monotony, despite the pious protests of the upper classes and the government that the poor were squandering their allowances.

Orwell's approach to socialism required him to investigate not only the conditions of unemployment in the industrial North, but also those of employment. Chapter II of *The Road to Wigan Pier* opens, like Conrad's *Victory*, with the observation that the modern world is built on coal. The miner is "a sort of grimy caryatid upon whose shoulders nearly everything that is not grimy is supported."[4] Practically everything we do, Orwell says later, "from eating an ice to crossing the Atlantic, and from baking a loaf to writing a novel, involves the use of coal, directly or indirectly. . . ."[5] We, therefore, ought to know something about coal mining. For Orwell, this meant going down into the mines and watching the miners get the coal out of the ground. Everyone, he says, ought to see a coal mine and see it when the fillers are at work on the coal face. To do this is difficult, because a visitor is a nuisance at this time, but at any other time he will get the wrong impression.

> On a Sunday, for instance, a mine seems almost peaceful.   The time to go there is when the machines are roaring and the air is black with coal dust, and when you can actually see what the miners have to do.   At these times the place is like hell, or at any rate like my own mental picture of hell.   Most of the things one imagines in hell are there—heat, noise, confusion, foul air, darkness, and, above all, unbearably cramped space.   Everything except the fire, for there is no fire down there except the feeble beams of Davy lamps and electric torches which scarcely penetrate the clouds of coal dust.[6]

Orwell descended to more than one mine on workdays in the "cage" (a dangerous business in itself at the time), "traveled" with the miners to the face (running at a fast clip, bending forward in the low galleries, sometimes for miles), and watched them dynamite the face and shovel the coal onto the conveyor belts. It is humiliating, he says, to watch coal miners at work.

> It raises in you a momentary doubt about your own status as an "intellectual" and a superior person generally.   For it is brought home to you . . . that it is only because miners sweat their guts out that superior persons can remain superior.   You and I and the editor of the *Times Lit. Supp.,* and the Nancy poets and the Archbishop of Canterbury and Comrade X, author of *Marxism for*

Infants—all of us really owe the comparative decency of our lives to poor drudges working underground, blackened to the eyes, with their throats full of coal dust, driving their shovels forward with arms and belly muscles of steel.[7]

And what was the miner's reward? When Orwell made his investigation, a miner who was working steadily earned scarcely enough to live on. If he was injured or succumbed to one of the occupational disorders of minors, like nystagmus, he received a pension which was a miserable fraction of his wages. From a pensioned minor in one of the boarding houses where he stayed, Orwell learned about the procedure of collecting pensions. Each week the miner had to go to the mine at a time fixed by the company. This meant, in the first place, that he had to spend sixpence on bus fares; and when he got to the mine, he might have to wait around half the afternoon. Of course, the company could just have easily paid the miner by check, but that would have been treating him like a member of the middle classes.

Orwell considered that the constant inconveniences and indignities to which the worker was subjected under capitalism had a significantly suppressive effect and explained certain differences, some real and some supposed, between the working classes and the other classes. From the beginning, Orwell says, the working man is forced into a passive role. He feels that a mysterious "they" have the power to stop him from doing all sorts of things. The middle-class man, on the other hand, believes that he can get some of the good things that he wants out of life. It is this difference in attitudes, Orwell insists, that explains why educated people come to the front in times of crisis. He denies that they are any more gifted than working men; he also denies that their education has any value. Their advantage is not that they have more brains than uneducated men, but that they have more cheek.

The Road to Wigan Pier is Orwell's strongest and most sustained attack on capitalism and the class system, his stoutest defense of the working man. Under the present system, Orwell says in effect, the life of the working man is bad enough; but if it were left to those who control the system to decide whether the system should not continue or the laboring man's life should be made worse, then the laboring man's life would be made worse. If coal could only be got out of the ground, as it once was, by women, crawling on their hands and knees and dragging the stuff after them in tubs attached by chains to harnesses around their waists, then it would be got out that way.

In *The Road to Wigan Pier,* however, as well as in other places, Orwell submitted that the working classes were not the only people whose lives demonstrated the necessity of establishing socialism in England. The whole middle class, he argued, suffered under capitalism. Compared with the lives of the poor, those of even the lower middle classes were, of course, fairly comfortable physically. Psychologically, however, they were far from comfortable. Middle-class incomes were no longer commensurate with middle-class traditions that dated from the prosperity of the late nineteenth century, and it was a strain to keep living as if they were. The typical middle-class man had to count the cost of luxuries and worry constantly about necessities—including the rent. Though Tories continued to speak in accents of horror about the plans of socialists to do away with the right of the English citizen to private property, the fact was that only a very small proportion of Englishmen owned any property. In *Coming Up for Air* George Bowling says that the people in his neighborhood merely think that they own their houses.

> As a matter of fact, in Ellesmere Road we don't own our houses even when we've finished paying for them. They're not freehold, only leasehold. . . . We're all . . . in the middle of paying for our houses and eaten up with the ghastly fear that something might happen before we've made the last payment. . . .[8]

World War II stimulated the English economy and decreased unemployment, as Orwell knew it would, yet the evils of capitalism that the War revealed were perhaps greater than the ones it remedied. Hitler's successes during the early stages of the War were, Orwell said, "a physical debunking of capitalism."[9] Why, after eight months of war, was the Army equipped to no more than a 1918 standard? Why did the British have only one plane when the Nazis had three and bayonets when the Nazis had tommy guns? Why was there a shortage of uniforms in one of the great wool-producing countries of the world? Because the interests of the country pulled in one direction and those of private corporations pulled in another. Tanks were needed, but automobiles were more profitable. It was common sense to keep strategic materials from a potential enemy, but the duty of any board of directors was to sell to the highest market and make money for the stockholders.

Even after the War was well under way, said Orwell, the struggle between private profit and public necessity continued, as advertisements in the newspapers strikingly illustrated. On the same page that the Government appealed to readers to save their money, manufacturers coaxed them to spend it on chocolates and cold cream. At the same time that workers were being asked to put in longer hours, the wealthy were running ads for butlers. "Everywhere," Orwell wrote in 1941, "privilege is squandering good will."[10] The Home Guard was rigged so that only the monied classes could get commands; the very rationing system was fixed to favor the rich.

The War brought into greater prominence what Orwell considered to be the most significant fact in English history during the past seventy-five years: the decay of ability in the ruling classes that made English statesmen help Spain to become Fascist in 1936 and facilitate the sale of arms to Italy in 1939—that made them, in fact, do the wrong thing at every turn. What was the cause of this decay? Before the thirties, Orwell said, it was clear to thousands of people that the ruling classes had ceased to be of any real use to England; their functions had been taken over by managers and technicians. But the ruling classes could not admit to themselves that they had ceased to be useful.

> Had they done that, they would have had to abdicate. . . . After all, they belonged to a class with a certain tradition. . . . They had to *feel* themselves true patriots, even while they plundered their countrymen. Clearly there was only one escape for them—into stupidity. They could keep society in its existing shape only by being *unable* to grasp that any improvement was possible. Difficult though this was, they achieved it, largely by fixing their eyes on the past and refusing to notice the changes that were going on round them.[11]

This deliberate stupidity, Orwell said, explained, among other things, the fake feudalism that has driven the better workers off the land, the ossification of the public schools, and the series of disasters that has characterized the early stages of every war that England has fought since the 1850's.

England, said Orwell, was like a large family run by its oldest and least competent members:

It has rich relations who have to be kow-towed to and poor
relations who are horribly sat upon, and there is a deep conspiracy
of silence about the source of the family income.   It is a family
in which the young are generally thwarted and most of the power
is in the hands of irresponsible uncles and bed-ridden aunts.[12]

Yet these classes, though incompetent and irresponsible, were not
wicked. Orwell did not waste any time drawing cartoons of sinister
men with monocles and top hats. Simon, Hoare, and Chamberlain,
he said, had an instinct to come to ultimate terms with Hitler, but
this would have meant breaking up the Empire and selling their
people into slavery, and they were not corrupt enough to do that.
The willingness of the upper classes to die for their country demon-
strates their moral soundness. Their chief fault is that they are
simply unteachable. "Only when their money and power are gone
will the younger among them begin to grasp what century they are
living in."[13]

ii. THE IMPEDIMENTS TO SOCIALISM

The unequal distribution of wealth and the atrophy of the ruling classes clearly called, Orwell thought, for a reorganization of English society. Naturally, the reorganization would be opposed by those who enjoyed special benefits under the existing system. In addition to this resistance there was another kind, paradoxical and perhaps peculiar to the English class system. Since World War I, Orwell believed, the deterioration of the ruling classes had been accompanied by a deterioration of the upper-middle class—the military, professional, and official classes, who did not own land but who "kept up a semi-aristocratic outlook."[14] Even before the War there were discrepancies between their incomes and their outlook. For instance, they knew how to wear clothes and how to order dinners, but many of them could not afford a really good tailor or restaurant. Between wars they nearly exhausted themselves keeping up appearances, and so they became more conscious of poverty than all but the poorest of the working classes were. As these sections of the middle classes got economically closer to the working classes, they got more hostile. Their attitude became one "of sniggering superiority punctuated by bursts of vicious hatred."[15] One thing, then, to remember about classes is that they do not correspond to economic strata.

In *Coming Up for Air* Orwell provides a serio-comic illustration of the fact that between classes which are economically very close there may be a deep cultural gulf. George Bowling comes from the small shop-keeping class, and his wife Hilda from the "poverty-stricken officer" class, and when George visits Hilda's home in Ealing, he steps into what is almost a foreign country (as Hilda would have done if she had visited George's family in Lower Binfield). Neither of them has any idea of what the other is really like, and after their marriage George is constantly irritated by Hilda's crust-wiping, while Hilda is chronically worried about George's rather nonchalant attitude toward money. ("But, George, it's very *serious*! I don't know what we're going to *do*! I don't know where the money's coming from! You don't seem to realize how serious it *is*!")[16]

Since the schoolmaster and the small-holder will tend to think of the garage mechanic and the coal-miner as "proletarians," since the office worker will think of the manual worker as a greasy, muscular fellow without proper sensibilities and will become suspicious of any talk of leveling classes, since, in short, the poorer members of the middle classes tend to dislike and fear the working classes, and since the upper classes derive their attitudes toward the worker from the middle classes, a greater unification of classes is a prerequisite of socialism.

Orwell recognized that the obstacles in the way of unification were numerous and deeply-rooted. First of all, there was the obstacle of accent and manners. When Orwell was a child, he was forbidden to play with the plumber's children because they would ruin his accent. If he grew up with the wrong accent, he might lose the advantages and privileges of his class. This sort of childhood conditioning affects in later life even those who wish to repudiate advantage and privilege. Why, asks Orwell, does an educated man who identifies himself with the working classes "take such pains to drink his soup silently? It can only be because he feels in his heart that proletarian manners are disgusting."[17] In his youth Orwell himself was an excellent illustration of the split between political theory and personal sympathy in the middle classes: ". . . at the age of seventeen or eighteen I was both a snob and a revolutionary."[18] He was against authority, read Shaw and Wells, and called himself a socialist. Yet he did not have the slightest idea of what he meant by socialism, and he had no idea that the worker was a human being. Looking back on these years, he had a feeling that he had "spent half the time denouncing the capitalistic system and the other half in raging over the insolence of bus-conductors."[19]

Another obstacle to unification, Orwell thought, was the fact that a great many people who had never been to public schools or universities themselves believed that the educated Englishman was a better sort of person than the uneducated Englishman. During his tramping period Orwell discovered the terrific force which the idea of the gentleman exerts throughout the Western world, but perhaps especially in England. When tramps stop for the night at the casual ward of a workhouse, they are supervised (or were at the time) by an official called the tramp major, usually a workhouse pauper himself. As soon as the tramp major at Lower Binfield learned that Orwell was a gentleman (as Orwell's listing his occupation as journalist indicated to him), he began to treat him with special consideration and to regard his plight with special regret.

Orwell, however, believed that the educated man who has come down in the world all the way to the tramp level is actually less to be pitied than the uneducated man who has slipped only a short distance to reach the tramp level. When the latter loses his work, he has no resources against the deadening ennui of idleness. He cannot, like the educated man, read, observe, and speculate. Once Orwell asked a tramp friend to go into a library with him; the friend declined, saying that the sight of all the bloody print made him sick.

A greater barrier between classes than manners, accent, or the conception of the gentleman is a belief "summed up in four frightful words": "The lower classes smell."[20] Nowadays, Orwell says, few people admit to this belief, but he finds a remarkably candid expression of it in Somerset Maugham's *On a Chinese Screen*. Maugham is describing the arrival of an important Chinese official at a small inn. He raises a great commotion and insults everyone in order to assert his superiority. Five minutes later he is eating dinner with the baggage coolies. In the Western world, Maugham says, this would be unthinkable.

> In the West we are divided from our fellows by our sense of smell. . . . I do not blame the working man because he stinks, but stink he does. It makes social intercourse difficult to persons of sensitive nostril. The matutinal tub divides the classes more effectually than birth, wealth or education.[21]

In his own day, says Orwell, middle-class children were brought up to believe that the lower classes were unclean—as, indeed, lacking the means to be otherwise, they often were. He supplies some horrendous childhood memories:

> You watched a great sweaty navvy walking down the road with his pick over his shoulder; you looked at his discolored shirt and his corduroy trousers stiff with the dirt of a decade; you thought of those nests and layers of greasy rags below, and, under all, the unwashed body, brown all over (that was how I used to imagine it) with its strong, bacon-like reek.[22]

This is bad enough, and yet Orwell suggests that between the upper and middle classes and the lower there is something less tangible than bathtubs but more formidable: a myth. The other classes attribute to the lower not only a superficial dirtiness, but an essential difference. ". . . even 'lower-class' people whom you knew to be quite clean—servants, for instance—were faintly unappetizing.

The smell of their sweat, the very texture of their skins, were mysteriously different from yours."[23]

Of all the wrong-headed beliefs about the lower classes that the other classes hold, this belief that they are physically repulsive is the hardest to outgrow.

> For no feeling of like or dislike is quite so fundamental as a *physical* feeling. Race-hatred, religious-hatred, difference of education, of temperament, of intellect, even difference of moral code can be got over; but physical repulsion cannot.[24]

The myth among the middle class that the lower classes are physically repulsive has its equivalent in a myth among educated proletarians that the other classes are effete. The proletarian who has struggled up to a stratum where he expects to discover a greater intellectual refinement discovers, instead, hollowness, bloodlessness, deadness.

> This at any rate is what he says. . . . D. H. Lawrence, who was sincere, whatever else he may not have been, expresses the same thought over and over again. It is curious how he harps on the idea that the English bourgeoisie are all *dead,* or at least gelded.[25]

Orwell quotes Lawrence's poem about the young man who climbed to the top of the tree but did not admire the other young men that he found there because they had all been emasculated, and then observes:

> Lawrence tells me that because I have been to a public school I am a eunuch. . . . I can produce medical evidence to the contrary, but what good will that do? Lawrence's condemnation remains. If you tell me I am a scoundrel I may mend my ways, but if you tell me I am a eunuch you are tempting me to hit back in any way that seems feasible. If you want to make an enemy of a man, tell him that his ills are incurable.[26]

There are, then, errors on both sides, and each class will have to work hard to overcome its prejudices about the other.

Yet Orwell feels that the effort on the part of some upper- and middle-class enthusiasts to bring about an understanding between classes overnight is itself an obstacle to understanding. He scorned the summer schools where middle-class socialists and proletarians are supposed to be brotherly, and the summer camps where

> public-school boys and boys from the slums are supposed to mix
> on exactly equal terms, and *do* mix for the time being, rather
> like the animals in one of those "Happy Family" cages where a
> dog, a cat, two ferrets, a rabbit and three canaries preserve an
> armed truce while the showman's eye is upon them.[27]

To make socialism succeed, Orwell thought, the English upper and
middle classes would have to make haste slowly. And if a man had
an invincible sense of superiority, it would be better to say so, as
George Saintsbury did, than to pretend to democratic sentiments.

The socialist movement faced grave problems, Orwell thought,
not only in the system of classes, but also in the composition of its
own membership. A large class of socialists, he believed, consisted
of the worst sort of cranks. His belief that cranks of one kind or
another were hindering socialism just by being socialists moved him
to a fierceness and unfairness not characteristic of him:

> One sometimes gets the impression that the mere words Socialism
> and Communism draw towards them with magnetic force every
> fruitjuice-drinker, nudist, sandal-wearer, sex-maniac, Quaker, "Na-
> ture Cure" quack, pacifist and feminist in England.[28]

To keep away from socialism because socialists are not attractive is
not, of course, a rational kind of conduct; but thousands of possible
converts, says Orwell, meeting the more outlandish types of socialists can hardly be blamed if they conclude that there is no room in
the movement for them.

Other socialists who, in Orwell's opinion, repelled possible converts were those who subscribed to the cult of Russia. These people
crusaded for socialism in a Marxist jargon about as intelligible to
the average working man as a textbook of higher mathematics.
Orwell recalled one of them whom he had heard addressing a
working-class audience.

> His speech was the usual bookish stuff, full of long sentences and
> parentheses and "Notwithstanding" and "Be that as it may," beside
> the usual "ideology and "class-consciousness" and "proletarian soli-
> darity" and all the rest of it. After him a Lancashire working man
> got up and spoke to the crowd in their broad lingo. There was
> not much doubt which of the two was nearer to his audience.[29]

The tendency to despotism was another repellent quality that
Orwell observed in English socialists. Most English Marxists, he

said, would not even agree with his primary definition of socialists: those who wish to see tyranny overthrown. (Some of them became extremely indignant when Orwell referred to Russian commissars as half-gramophones-half-gangsters.) Some socialists who did not subscribe to the cult of Russia also had a tyrant's instincts. To be sure, their despotism was of a benevolent and non-violent kind, but despotism still. They were not working for a democratic socialism, but for a system in which clever people imposed their notions of the good society on less clever ones. These intellectuals dismissed as anachronistic the emotional side of life which includes patriotism, hero-worship, and a sense of tradition. Actually, says Orwell, these emotions are the forces that move the ordinary man. The ordinary man might possibly accept a dictatorship of the proletariat, but he will never accept a dictatorship of prigs. Indeed, the mere idea of a dictatorship of socialistic prigs may drive him toward Fascism, which appeals to the emotions that the prigs dismiss. Moreover, insofar as these socialists succeed in creating the impression that socialism leaves national cultures behind on the way to Utopia, they not only repel the ordinary man, they drive some of the ablest literary men to the Right. This, Orwell says, explains the position of Pound, Eliot, and Wyndham Lewis.

iii.   THE FORCES IN FAVOR OF SOCIALISM

That there were deep divisions between classes in England and that various crackpot and pernicious doctrines were touted under the name of socialism were, Orwell thought, formidable difficulties in the way of socialism. But he also thought that if socialism were presented to the English in the proper light, they could make such a success of a socialistic society as few other countries in the world could.

A socialist revolution in England, Orwell believed, would be a bloodless one because of the English sense of solidarity and decency. Strong as their consciousness of belonging to a particular class was, it was not so strong as their consciousness of being Englishmen.

> England [Orwell wrote in 1941] is the most class-ridden country under the sun. It is a land of snobbery and privilege. . . . But in any calculation about it one has got to take into account its emotional unity. . . . It is the only great country in Europe that is not obliged to drive hundreds of thousands of its nationals into exile or the concentration camp.[30]

If the English could be made to see the urgency of socialism, Orwell thought, they would work for its establishment with the same sort of unanimity with which they worked for victory during the war.

Gentleness, Orwell believed, was the most marked characteristic of English civilization. It was the gentleness of the atmosphere that most struck him when he crossed the Channel.

> It was queer after Paris; everything was so much clearner and quieter. . . . One missed the . . . noisy, festering life of the back streets, and the armed men clattering through the squares. The crowds were better dressed and the faces comelier and milder and more alike, without that fierce individuality and malice of the French. There was less drunkenness, and less dirt, and less quarreling. . . .[31]

Orwell elsewhere describes similar scenes and adds that they are typical of England. The passages are a sort of prosaic equivalent of these lyrical passages in the novels of E. M. Forster which invoke the spirit of England; and the interesting thing is that it is Forster who, like the Shakespeare of the historical plays, celebrates the splendor and strength of England and Orwell, the admirer of Kipling, who praises its peacefulness. Above all things, Orwell says, the English hate militarism, "the swaggering officer type, the jingle of spurs and the crash of boots."[32] If the goose-step were introduced into the British Army, the people on the street would laugh it out again.

Even the harsh aspects of English civilization, such as some of the anachronisms in the criminal law, go to show the respect that the English have for law and order. The law is something above the state as well as the individual. It is incorruptible, however cruel and stupid it may be. It allows men to be flogged and children to be submitted to worse barbarities. "Still, if Al Capone were in an English jail, it would not be for evasion of income tax."[33] Because of their respect for law and order the English are suspicious of the conspiratorial and dislike any movement characterized by militance. They have refused to adopt the attitudes that go with modern power politics. Instead of developing a world view, they have retained their patriotism. Instead of acquiring a twentieth-century political theory, they have kept their common decency. In their way they have remained more Christian than any other people in Europe: they have continued to believe that might does not make right. "Even the most drastic changes," said Orwell, "will have to happen peacefully . . . and everyone except the 'lunatic fringes' of the various political parties is aware of this."[34] For the English have always avoided violence whenever possible. They have, on the whole, conducted their internal politics in a decent and humane way, and they have kept a huge empire together with a remarkably small number of armed men. They have retained a habit which is becoming rare in the modern world, the habit of not killing one another. If any nation can, they can make a revolution without bloodshed and abolish poverty without destroying liberty.

iv. THE RESERVATIONS ABOUT SOCIALISM

Passionately as Orwell longed for socialism, he was conspicuously cool toward some of the corollaries of socialism: increased mechanization, wider control by the government, greater uniformity in the lives of the citizens. In his attitude toward the machine he tried to steer a course between two extreme attitudes which he encountered among socialists. Those who held the first view identified the improvement of society with the multiplication of machines. They waxed enthusiastic over a Wellsian world and saw no danger in the machine except as it might be used for destructive purposes.

> Barring wars and unforeseen disasters, the future is envisaged as an ever more rapid march of mechanical progress; machines to save work, machines to save thought, machines to save pain, hygiene, efficiency, organization, more hygiene, more efficiency, more organization, more machines. . . .[35]

Those who held the alternate extreme view regarded mechanization not as the central doctrine of the true religion, but as the major heresy of the modern world. Some of these people yearned sentimentally for medieval crafts and guilds; some were what Orwell liked to call "literary gents," jealous of the prestige of the scientist and the engineer; some were esthetes in shuddering recoil from factories and industrial plants.

Orwell's own position was a compromise. He knew that the machine was necessary to socialism, if not in the way that some of the machine-worshippers imagined, since the mass of people must sweat to provide comfort for a few in any society that is not highly mechanized. However, he saw dangers in the machine even beyond its possibilities for war. Therefore, he said, we should accept the machine, but grudgingly and suspiciously, as one accepts a drug. He was not always able, however, to maintain this compromise, because he had too violent an anti-mechanical bias. Sometimes the machine seemed to him not merely a dangerous drug, but a downright poison. He set up an arbitrary dichotomy between the machine and physical, mental, and moral degeneracy on the one hand, and nature and virtue and health on the other. He seemed to regard the admiration that many people have for a piece of machinery *per se* as a corruption of wholesome human response, and the passion that some men have for inventing new machines and improving old ones as a kind of sinister dementia. Seeing in his mind's eye thousands upon thousands of engineers contriving to produce better and better machines, he could imagine the same world of the future that the Wellsians imagined. To him, however, it was only a new world, not a brave one. It was a world in which nothing went wrong. Since there was no danger in it, there was no courage; since there was no need for exertion, there was no strength; since there were no difficulties, there was no resourcefulness. The machine, which had begun by raising men from a sub-human level by releasing them from drudgery, would eventually reduce them to a sub-human world once more by robbing them of effort.

In the present world Orwell thought that he saw evidence that the machine was not only lightening the work of some men, but taking all of it away from them. "So much the better," Orwell could, apparently, hear the machine-worshipper saying. "All work is a nuisance." But for Orwell work was not a nuisance; it was a necessity. "For man is not, as the vulgarer hedonists seem to suppose, a kind of walking stomach; he has also got a hand, an eye and a brain. Cease to use your hands and you have lopped off a huge chunk of your consciousness."[36] Orwell gratuitously assumes that men really will cease to use their hands to do any job that can be done by a machine. Suppose, he says, that machinery frees a gang of men from overlong hours of ditch-digging and that they wish to do some carpenter work in their leisure. They will find that the machine has done that for them, too. Instead of making a table, they have only to assemble the pieces. As to the idea that they can go ahead and make the table by hand from the beginning anyhow, Orwell says that whenever a machine is available, it will be used. People just do not do things the hard way. A man will not walk from the country to London when buses are passing him every quarter of an hour. What Orwell forgets is that the man who rides to London every day of the week so that he can be at work on time may walk there on the week end simply for the fun of it. In an age made more convenient, softer, and safer by machinery, people will cling to inconveniences, difficulties, and dangers as they cling to privileges. They go safely up a mountain in a machine and then go dangerously down on skis.

Orwell, however, insists on regarding nature and the machine not as complementary, but as antagonistic. Nature is essentially good and the machine is essentially evil, and so we should all rally round natural phenomena, which will somehow enable us to forestall the folly and wickedness which will otherwise overcome us. In "Some Thoughts on the Common Toad" he says,

> I think that by retaining one's childhood love of such things as trees, fish, butterflies and—to return to my first instance—toads, one makes a peaceful and decent future a little more probable, and that by preaching the doctrine that nothing is to be admired except steel and concrete, one merely makes it a little surer that human beings will have no outlet for their surplus energy except in hatred and leader-worship.[37]

This is not the only place in which Orwell equates the machine and its products with the particular evils of our time. The equation is one of the motifs of *Coming Up for Air*.

> I remembered [George Bowling says] a bit I'd read in the paper somewhere about these . . . factories in Germany where everything's made of something else. . . . That's the way we're going nowadays. Everything slick and streamlined. . . . Celluloid, rubber, chromium-steel everywhere, arc-lamps blazing all night, glass roofs over your head, radios all playing the same tune, no vegetation left, everything cemented over, mock turtles grazing under the neutral fruit-trees.[38]

George has just gone into the kind of milk-bar where more money is spent on the decorations than the food to get a snack. When he bites into a frankfurter, he finds that it is stuffed with stinking fish. "It gave me the feeling that I'd bitten into the modern world and discovered what it was really made of."[39] In fact, Orwell thinks that food is one of the best indexes to the madness of a mechanized world. Most of the hops in England, George has heard, are not made into beer, but are turned into chemicals; and other chemicals are made into beer.

Of course, Orwell had no wish to return to the Victorian Age, but if its politics had been different, he would have found the time altogether preferable to his own. He was attracted to the socialism that the twentieth century makes possible, but repelled by the chromium-plated culture that goes with it; he was repelled by the political system of the nineteenth century, but attracted by Victorian culture. Although he looked hopefully forward to a time when most of England's commerce would be nationalized, he looked regretfully backward to a time in which some of it at least was conducted by Fezziwigs in an atmosphere of Dickensian coziness. George Bowling worked eleven hours a day at Grimmet's grocery store when he was a young fellow, but he thinks with nostalgia of that time of his life.

Coming Up for Air is, indeed, a study in nostalgia; it is the equivalent of Mark Twain's autobiographical writings and H. L. Mencken's *Happy Days*. With the same mixture of gratification and regret that Twain and Mencken re-create life in Hannibal and Baltimore at an earlier time, Orwell re-creates life in Lower Binfield.

Orwell's nostalgia, however, is partly for a life and time he never actually knew. His hero is ten years older than Orwell himself and the son of a small shopkeeper. Yet the life of a shopkeeper's son in an English market town at the beginning of the century (George Bowling was born in 1893) is vividly and convincingly described. There are excellent sections on the routines of the shop and the household, the politics, pastimes, and superstitions. There are accounts of the meals ("Enormous meals—boiled beef and dumplings, roast beef and Yorkshire, boiled mutton and capers, pig's head, apple pie, spotted dog and jam roly-poly—with grace before and after")[40] and even catalogues of the sweets:

> Most sweets were four ounces a penny, and there was even some stuff called Paradise mixture, mostly broken sweets from other bottles, which was six. Then there were Farthing Everlastings, which were a yard long and couldn't be finished inside half an hour.[41]

Since *Coming Up for Air* derives in part from *Kipps* and *The History of Mr. Polly* (starting with his school days, Orwell read most of H. G. Wells), it is worth noticing how Wells's treatment of the same material differs from Orwell's and how it resembles it. Wells, who was in fact the son of a small shopkeeper and was actually apprenticed to a firm of drapers at the age of thirteen, draws a grimmer picture of the life of the small retailer and the apprentice than Orwell does. Until he comes into money, Kipps works not eleven but fourteen hours a day in the shop, eats food less designed to provide nourishment than to save his master money, sleeps in a bed that he tries to keep warm with the help of his overcoat and old newspapers. Until he inherits his small legacy, Mr. Polly leads a similarly miserable life. When he buys his own shop, his leisure increases, but so does his boredom. In place of at least a few amiable companions he has a wife with just enough intelligence to have trapped him into marriage. And instead of being ill paid, he is on the verge of bankruptcy.

But there is still more sheer fun in Wells's novels than in *Coming Up for Air*. Scenes like Mr. Polly's wedding are almost pure Dickens, Uncle Pentstemon is a Dickensian comic character, and Polly himself, with his elaborate mispronunciation of an ambitious vocabulary, is something of a Dickensian grotesque. In Polly there is less awareness and less responsibility than in George Bowling. Polly has no understanding of the causes behind the world from which he recoils; his rebellion is not so much deliberate as desperate, like his fight with Uncle Jim, the terror of the Potwell Inn. In the end Polly becomes a kind of knight, as he dreamed of doing; if he does not rescue a beautiful maiden, he rescues an old lady from a burning building and drives the dreadful Jim away from the Potwell. Polly, however, is no perfect knight. He has set the fire himself; he swindles a life insurance company as well as a fire insurance company; he deserts his wife. Partly by a refusal to obey the rules and partly by a sort of blind flailing out, the little man saves himself from the forces that have almost smothered him. *The History of Mr. Polly* is an anarchistic comedy.

But the books are not so dissimilar as all this might make them seem to be. If the life of the small shopkeeper sounds more prosperous in *Coming Up for Air* than in *The History of Mr. Polly,* it is because George Bowling's father is more fortunate than the average (George sees shops going broke all over Lower Binfield because they cannot compete with the new chains) and because he deludes himself into thinking that the decline in his trade is only temporary. And if Wells knows the harsh lot of the apprentice in the nineteenth century better than Orwell does, he shares Orwell's nostalgia for the English countryside and the rural sports of the time. In *Kipps* there are accounts of holidays spent running about on the beach, swimming in the sea, playing smugglers, racing through the fields, and watching windmills. And in *The History of Mr. Polly,* as in Orwell's novel, it is the English countryside that wakes the hero, that causes him to come up for air.

Even the dirt of the old days had a kind of appeal to Orwell when he considered the coldness that goes with the streamlined cleanliness of the new ones. Discussing the problem of slum-clearing, he said repeatedly, in the sort of metaphor that is rare in his writing, that he was torn two ways by it. He had seen, he said, too many slums to feel "Chestertonian raptures" about them, but he said it right after he had been talking exactly as Chesterton talked about slums. The procedure of delousing people and their belongings before moving them into new quarters has, he admitted, its points. But it is the kind of thing that "makes you wish that the word 'hygiene' could be dropped out of the dictionary."[42] Indeed, Orwell shared Chesterton's hatred of hygiene so much that he adopted for the moment the worst side of Chesterton's style, cracking silly epigrams in a good cause: ". . . the price of liberty is not so much eternal vigilance as eternal dirt."[43] When, in *Down and Out in Paris and London,* he is talking about the different kinds of lodging houses available to tramps in London, he says that the Salvation Army hostels would appeal only to people who put cleanliness above everything else. The ordinary lodging houses are stuffy, noisy, and dirty, but they are redeemed by their "laissez-faire atmosphere and the warm, home-like kitchens."[44]

"Laissez-faire" and "home-like" suggest another implication of socialism that Orwell regretted, that the greater the degree of socialism, the greater the degree of control the state must exercise over matters like housing. Even under the Council housing projects of the present, certain restrictions are clearly necessary (people cannot, for example, keep pigeons). When the slum-dweller or the coal-miner moves into a Council house, he does not lose any of the central liberties of British tradition, but Orwell deplored the fact that he had to lose even some peripheral ones. Orwell thought (again like Chesterton) that a certain amount of sloppiness was necessary for a healthy society, and he considered that the motive of many a socialist was simply an excessive sense of order: he objected to society as it was, not because it was miserable or because it was not free, but just because it was untidy; he wished to transform the sprawling expansiveness of normal human beings into the neatness of a chessboard.

Orwell saw in the America of the nineteenth century an even better example of a free and healthy civilization than in the England of the same period. The buoyant and confident quality of American life at the time, not only on the frontier but also in the East, was reflected, he thought, in some of the popular books. "The people in *Helen's Babies* or *Little Women* may be mildly ridiculous, but they are uncorrupted. They have something that is perhaps best described as integrity or good morale. . . ."[45] But some of the popular American books of the present reflect a very different sort of attitude toward life, as does that area of British literature which has been affected by American. Instead of being gentle and naive, they are tough and sophisticated. ". . . Freud and Machiavelli have reached the outer suburbs."[46] The remark itself sounds like a Freudian slip. "Marx and Machiavelli" would have been another matter, but why couple a power-politician with a physician, a destructive with a healing influence? Because Orwell is thinking not of Freud's therapy, but of his theories. Personally, Freud was probably more puritanical than Orwell, but Freudian doctrine has destroyed the taboos and taken away the innocence of the nineteenth century.

Orwell's George Bowling is neither puritanical nor religious, but he, too, regrets the passage from a world of innocence to a world of sophistication, and from a world which had more faith than efficiency to one which has more efficiency than faith. But even the efficiency of the modern world, George considers, is a delusion, since it leads to a loss of well-being, not a gain. The more violently people dash about, the less alive they feel. The heady atmosphere of the sophisticated twentieth century is ultimately less invigorating than the pure atmosphere of the naive nineteenth. Walking down the Strand one day, George falls into a reverie and finds himself back in the church at Lower Binfield at the beginning of the century.

> Of course, such impressions don't last more than a few seconds. A moment later it was as though I'd opened my eyes again, and I was forty-five and there was a traffic jam in the Strand. But it had left a kind of after-effect behind. Sometimes when you come out of a train of thought you feel as if you were coming up from deep water, but this time it was the other way about, it was as though it was back in 1900 that I'd been breathing real air. Even now, with my eyes open, so to speak, all those bloody fools hustling to and fro, and the posters and the petrol-stink and the roar of the engines, seemed to me less real than Sunday morning in Lower Binfield thirty-eight years ago.[47]

Later, driving through the territory that he covers for his insurance company, George stops at the roadside to look at the winter wheat and smell the air and pick a few of the primroses that cover a spot of ground on the edge of the field. Beside the patch of flowers he sees a small pool and the embers of a wood fire left by a tramp, and all at once he feels happy and really alive. Being alive is "a feeling inside you, a kind of peaceful feeling, and yet it's like a flame."[48] In the old days, when people took time just to walk around and look at things, they had this feeling. For George, however, the chief symbol of the old time is not primroses or fires, but fishing. The boyhood section of *Coming Up for Air* has a chapter on fishing, beside which, George says, everything he has ever done since has been a disappointment. There are fine accounts of whole days spent at the pools around Lower Binfield and detailed explanations of tackle and the right kinds of bait for various fish. Even the names of the fish are recited with a sort of enchantment. George, in fact, speaks of the "magic" of fishing, and, in effect, he speaks of the mystique. But the most fabulous thing of all is the pool which George discovers on the grounds of Binfield House, surrounded by a thick growth of trees and underbrush, forgotten by everybody, and filled with huge carp. On the day of the discovery, however, George does not have a strong enough line for the fish; and he never gets back to the pool again. In fact, for all his passion and knowledge, George has not fished anywhere for thirty years. He has grown up into a world in which, like other people, he does everything except the thing that he really wants to do. The great fish swim through his daydreams as they do through the pool, getting larger and larger with the years, but he spends his Bank Holidays anywhere but at Binfield House. Once, during the War, he and a friend come upon a pond filled with carp and resolve to catch some of them even though they have no proper equipment. Orwell develops their strategems to evade the sergeant and their frenzied efforts to improvise the necessary gear into a nice little piece of suspense. Finally, when, at the cost of cutting and burning their fingers, they have succeeded in making a usable hook, and are ready to go after the fish, they get orders to move in twenty minutes. They never see the pool again. "I expect," George says, "it got poisoned with mustard gas later on."[49]

Standing by the primrose and the embers, George suddenly decides that he will go back to Lower Binfield. He will see the old places and breathe the old air, and—best of all—he will catch some of the great carp. He has just won seventeen pounds on a horse, plenty for a week's visit, and so he hides the money from his wife, lies to his employers, and sneaks away to his native village. But he cannot, of course, really go back to Lower Binfield. His father's place of business has been turned into Wendy's Tea Shoppe. The name Bowling means nothing at all to the desk-clerk at the now hideously modern hotel. As for the pool where the carp once swam, it has become a rubbish dump. On one level of his mind George has always known that he could not get back. "Where are the great fish?" he has repeatedly asked himself, and the phrase is a sort of "Where are the snows of yesteryear?" And Orwell not only knows that it is impossible to go back; he also knows exactly what George would be going back to if he could. He did not imagine that the whole history of the nineteenth century was something written by Louisa May Alcott; his reconstruction of the end of the Victorian Age in *Coming Up for Air* includes plenty of dunghills and blue-bottle flies, but not much lavender and lace. Far from being senti-mental or pious, George Bowling's recollections are often vulgar and irreverent: "The drunks are puking in the yard behind the George. Vicky's at Windsor, God's in heaven, Christ's on the cross, Jonah's in the whale. . . . ."[50] But despite the crudeness and blas-phemy of his language George's remarks are obviously a tribute to a time when all things were in their proper places. ". . . I tell you it was a good world to live in. I belong to it. So do you."[51] And so did a part of George Orwell.

Notes

CHAPTER 1

1 "Such, Such Were the Joys," *Such, Such Were the Joys* (New York: Harcourt, Brace & Company, 1953), pp. 50-51.

2 *Down and Out in Paris and London* (New York: Harcourt, Brace & Company, 1950), p. 142.

3 *Ibid.,* p. 181.

4 *Ibid.,* pp. 182-183.

5 *Ibid.,* p. 185.

6 *Ibid.,* p. 83.

7 "Looking Back on the Spanish War," *Such, Such Were the Joys,* p. 150.

8 *Down and Out in Paris and London,* p. 171.

9 *The Lion and the Unicorn* (London: Secker & Warburg, 1941), p. 16.

10 *The Road to Wigan Pier* (New York: Harcourt, Brace & Company, 1958), p. 178.

11 *A Clergyman's Daughter* (New York: Harcourt, Brace & Company, 1960), p. 35.

12 *Ibid.,* p. 32.

13 *Ibid.,* p. 27.

14 *Ibid.,* p. 12.

15 "Poetry and the Microphone," *Such, Such Were the Joys,* p. 116.

16 *Down and Out in Paris and London,* p. 141.

17 *Homage to Catalonia* (New York: Harcourt, Brace & Company, 1952), p. 199.

18 *Ibid.,* pp. 164-165.

19 *Animal Farm* (New York: Harcourt, Brace & Company, 1946), p. 34.

20 *Ibid.,* p. 115.

21 "Lear, Tolstoy and the Fool," *Shooting an Elephant* (New York: Harcourt, Brace & Company, 1950), p. 33.

22 *Ibid.*

23 *Ibid.,* p. 36.

24 *Ibid.*

25 "Charles Dickens," *Dickens, Dali and Others* (New York: Reynal & Hitchcock, 1946), p. 69.

[26] *Ibid.,* p. 65.

[27] *Ibid.,* p. 63.

[28] "Lear, Tolstoy and the Fool," p. 52.

[29] "George Orwell," *Principles and Persuasions* (New York: Harcourt, Brace & Company, 1957), p. 167.

[30] *Ibid.,* p. 169.

[31] *Ibid.,* p. 171.

[32] "Anthony West as Critic," *The New Republic,* CXXXVI (April 15, 1957), p. 18.

[33] *Principles and Persuasions,* p. viii.

[34] "Anthony West as Critic," p. 18.

[35] "George Orwell," p. 174.

[36] *Ibid.,* p. 164.

[37] "Such, Such Were the Joys," p. 38.

[38] *Ibid.,* p. 29.

[39] *Ibid.,* p. 16.

[40] *Ibid.,* p. 40.

[41] *Ibid.,* p. 34.

[42] *Ibid.,* p. 51.

[43] *Ibid.,* p. 52.

[44] *Ibid.,* pp. 44-45.

[45] *Ibid.,* p. 57.

[46] *Ibid.,* p. 9.

[47] *Ibid.,* p. 32.

[48] *Ibid.,* p. 59.

[49] "Decency and Death," *Partisan Review,* XVII (May 1950), p. 518.

[50] "Orwell, or Two and Two Make Four," *The Writer and the Absolute* (London: Methuen & Company, Ltd., 1952), p. 162.

[51] *Ibid.*

[52] *The Road to Wigan Pier,* p. 17.

[53] *Homage to Catalonia,* p. 192.

[54] *The Road to Wigan Pier,* p. 177.

[55] *Ibid.,* p. 180.

[56] *Down and Out in Paris and London,* p. 62.

[57] *Ibid.,* p. 80.

[58] *Ibid.,* p. 121.

[59] *The Road to Wigan Pier,* p. 181.

[60] *Ibid.,* p. 183.

61 *Ibid.*, pp. 183-184.

62 *The Lion and the Unicorn,* p. 54.

63 "Decline of the English Murder," *Shooting an Elephant,* p. 160.

64 *A Clergyman's Daughter,* p. 85.

65 *Ibid.*, p. 16.

66 *Ibid.*, p. 297.

67 *Ibid.*, p. 279.

68 *Ibid.*, p. 318.

69 *Ibid.*, p. 320.

70 *Ibid.*, p. 299.

71 "Arthur Koestler," *Dickens, Dali and Others,* p. 200.

72 "Writers and Leviathan," *Such, Such Were the Joys,* p. 70.

73 "Inside the Whale," *Such, Such Were the Joys,* pp. 184-185.

74 *Homage to Catalonia,* p. 5.

75 Quoted by John Strachey, Introduction to *Studies in a Dying Culture* (London: John Lane, The Bodley Head, 1947), p. v.

76 "Looking Back on the Spanish War," pp. 135-136.

77 "Orwell, or Two and Two Make Four," p. 170.

78 *Ibid.*, p. 183.

79 "Inside the Whale," *Such, Such Were the Joys,* p. 195.

80 *Ibid.*, p. 196.

81 "Looking Back on the Spanish War," pp. 134-135.

82 *Ibid.*, p. 130.

83 "Politics and the English Language," *Shooting an Elephant,* pp. 77-78.

84 *Ibid.*, p. 88.

85 *Ibid.*, p. 92.

86 *Ibid.*, p. 86.

87 "Charles Dickens," pp. 74-75.

88 "Arthur Koestler," pp. 186-187.

89 "Rudyard Kipling," *Dickens, Dali and Others,* pp. 156-157.

90 "Raffles and Miss Blandish," *Dickens, Dali and Others,* p. 208.

91 *Ibid.*

92 *Ibid.*, p. 210.

93 *Ibid.*, p. 220.

94 "The Art of Donald McGill," *Dickens, Dali and Others,* p. 132.

95 *Ibid.*, pp. 135-136.

96 "Boys' Weeklies," *Dickens, Dali and Others,* p. 110.

[97] *Ibid.*, pp. 95-96.

[98] *Ibid.*, p. 101.

[99] *Ibid.*, pp. 110-111.

[100] *Ibid,* pp. 151-152.

[101] "In Defense of P. G. Wodehouse," *Dickens, Dali and Others,* p. 223.

[102] *Ibid.*, p. 242.

CHAPTER 2

[1] *Burmese Days* (New York: Harcourt, Brace & Company, 1950), p. 69.

[2] *Ibid,* p. 278

[3] *Ibid.*, p. 287.

[4] *Nineteen Eighty-Four* (New York: Harcourt, Brace & Company, 1949), p. 266.

[5] *Ibid.*, p. 224.

[6] *Ibid.*, p. 239

[7] *Ibid,* p. 243.

[8] *Ibid.*, p. 4.

[9] *Ibid,* pp. 167-168.

[10] *Ibid.*, pp. 294-295.

[11] "Looking Back on the Spanish War," *Such, Such Were the Joys* (New York: Harcourt, Brace & Company, 1953), pp. 141-142.

[12] *Darkness at Noon* (New York: The Macmillan Company, 1946), p. 117.

[13] *Nineteen Eighty-Four,* p. 215.

[14] *Ibid.*, p. 310.

[15] "Politics and the English Language," *Shooting an Elephant* (New York: Harcourt, Brace & Company, 1950), p. 87.

[16] *Nineteen Eighty-Four,* pp. 54-55.

[17] "Orwell, or Two and Two Make Four," *The Writer and the Absolute* (London: Methuen & Company, Ltd., 1952), p. 154.

18 "Second Thoughts on James Burnham," *Shooting an Elephant,* p. 137.

19 "Wells, Hitler and the World State," *Dickens, Dali and Others* (New York: Reynal & Hitchcock, 1946), p. 120.

20 "Second Thoughts on James Burnham," p. 139.

21 *Ibid.,* pp. 139-140.

22 "A Good Word for the Vicar of Bray," *Shooting an Elephant,* p. 170.

23 *Ibid.*

CHAPTER 3

1 *The Road to Wigan Pier* (New York: Harcourt, Brace & Company, 1958), p. 57.

2 *Ibid.,* p. 18.

3 *Ibid.,* p. 86.

4 *Ibid.,* p. 21.

5 *Ibid.,* p. 33.

6 *Ibid.,* pp. 21-22.

7 *Ibid.,* pp. 34-35.

8 *Coming Up for Air* (New York: Harcourt, Brace & Company, 1950), pp. 14-15.

9 *The Lion and the Unicorn* (London: Secker & Warburg, 1941), p. 60.

10 *Ibid.,* p. 74.

11 *Ibid.,* p. 74.

12 *Ibid.,* p. 35.

13 *Ibid.,* p. 44.

14 *The Road to Wigan Pier,* p. 155.

15 *Ibid.,* p. 156.

16 *Coming Up For Air,* p. 10.

17 *The Road to Wigan Pier,* p. 168.

18 *Ibid.,* p. 172.

19 *Ibid.,* p. 173.

20 *Ibid.,* p. 159.

21 *On a Chinese Screen* (New York: The George H. Doran Company, 1922), p. 142.

22 *The Road to Wigan Pier,* p. 160.

23 *Ibid.*

24 *Ibid.*

25 *Ibid.,* pp. 198-199.

[26] *Ibid.,* p. 200.

[27] *Ibid.,* p. 194.

[28] *Ibid.,* p. 206.

[29] *Ibid.,* pp. 207-208.

[30] *The Lion and the Unicorn,* p. 33.

[31] *Down and Out in Paris and London* (New York: Harcourt, Brace & Company, 1950), p. 134.

[32] *The Lion and the Unicorn,* p. 20.

[33] *The English People* (London: William Collins Sons & Company, Ltd., 1947), p. 16.

[34] *Ibid.,* p. 21.

[35] *The Road to Wigan Pier,* p. 225.

[36] *Ibid.,* p. 229.

[37] "Some Thoughts on the Common Toad," *Shooting an Elephant* (New York: Harcourt, Brace & Company, 1950), pp. 164-165.

[38] *Coming Up for Air,* pp. 27-28.

[39] *Ibid.,* p. 27.

[40] *Ibid.,* p. 57.

[41] *Ibid.,* p. 44.

[42] *The Road to Wigan Pier,* p. 73.

[43] *Ibid.,* p. 72.

[44] *Down and Out in Paris and London,* p. 210.

[45] "Riding Down from Bangor," *Shooting an Elephant,* p. 198.

[46] "Raffles and Miss Blandish," *Dickens, Dali and Others* (New York: Reynal & Hitchcock, 1946), p. 221.

[47] *Coming Up for Air,* p. 35.

[48] *Ibid.,* p. 193.

[49] *Ibid.,* p. 99.

[50] *Ibid.,* p. 36.

[51] *Ibid.*

A SELECTED BIBLIOGRAPHY

Books

Atkins, John. *George Orwell*. London: John Calder, 1954.

Brander, Laurence. *George Orwell*. London: Longmans, Green and Co., 1954.

Hollis, Christopher. *A Study of George Orwell*. London: Hollis and Carter, 1956.

Orwell, George. *Down and Out in Paris and London*. New York: Harcourt, Brace and Company, 1950. (First published in 1933.)

——————. *Burmese Days*. New York: Harcourt, Brace and Company, 1950. (First published in 1934.)

——————. *A Clergyman's Daughter*. New York: Harcourt, Brace and Company, 1960. (First published in 1935.)

——————. *Keep the Aspidistra Flying*. New York: Harcourt, Brace and Company, 1956. (First published in 1936.)

——————. *The Road to Wigan Pier*. New York: Harcourt, Brace and Company, 1958. (First published in 1937.)

——————. *Homage to Catalonia*. New York: Harcourt, Brace and Company, 1952. (First published in 1938.)

——————. *Coming Up for Air*. New York: Harcourt, Brace and Company, 1950. (First published in 1939.)

——————. *The Lion and the Unicorn*. London: Secker and Warburg, 1941. (First published in 1941.)

——————. *Animal Farm*. New York: Harcourt, Brace and Company, 1946. (First published in 1945.)

——————. *Dickens, Dali and Others*. New York: Reynal and Hitchcock, 1946. (First published in 1946.)

——————. *The English People*. London: Collins, 1947. (First published in 1947.)

——————. *Nineteen Eighty-Four*. New York: Harcourt, Brace and Company, 1949. (First published in 1949.)

——————. *Shooting an Elephant*. New York: Harcourt, Brace and Company, 1950. (First published in 1950.)

——————. *Such, Such Were the Joys*. New York: Harcourt, Brace and Company, 1953. (First published in 1953.)

Articles

Braybrooke, Neville. "Two Poverties." *The Commonweal,* LVIII (August 14, 1953), 459-461.

Cosman, Max. "George Orwell and the Autonomous Individual." Pacific Spectator, IX (Winter, 1955), 74-84.

——————. "Orwell's Terrain." *The Personalist,* XXXV (Winter,

Fyvel, T. R. "A Case for George Orwell?" *Twentieth Century,* CLX (September, 1956), 254-259.

Gleckner, Robert P. "1984 or 1948?" *College English,* XVIII (November, 1956), 95-99.

Howe, Irving. "Orwell: History as Nightmare." *American Scholar,* XXV (Spring, 1956), 193-207.

King, Carlyle. "The Politics of George Orwell." *University of Toronto Quarterly,* XXVI (October, 1956), 79-91.

Krutch, Joseph Wood. "Way of the Modern." *Saturday Review,* XXXVI (April 25, 1953), 19-20.

Lewis, Wyndham. "Orwell, or Two and Two Make Four." *The Writer and the Absolute.* London: Methuen, 1952, 153-193.

Potts, Paul. "Don Quixote on a Bicycle." *London Magazine,* IV (March, 1957), 39-47.

Rahv, Philip. "The Unfuture of Utopia." *Partisan Review,* XVI (July, 1949), 743-749.

Rieff, Phillip. "George Orwell and the Post-liberal Imagination." *Kenyon Review,* XVI (Summer, 1954), 49-70.

Rosenfeld, Isaac. "Decency and Death." *Partisan Review,* XVII (May, 1950), 514-518.

Rovere, Richard. "George Orwell." *New Republic,* CXXXV (September 10, 1956), 11-15.

Spender, Stephen. "One Man's Conscience." *New Republic,* CXXVIII (March 16, 1953), 18.

Trilling, Lionel. "George Orwell and the Politics of Truth." *Commentary,* XIII (March, 1952), 218-227.

Voorhees, Richard J. "George Orwell: Rebellion and Responsibility." *South Atlantic Quarterly,* LIII (October, 1954), 556-565.

————. "George Orwell as Critic." *Prairie Schooner,* XXVIII (Summer, 1954), 105-112.

————. "Orwell's Secular Crusade." *The Commonweal,* LXI (January 28, 1955), 448-451.

————. "Orwell and Power-Hunger." *Canadian Forum,* XXXVI (July, 1956), 79-80.

————. "*Nineteen Eighty-Four:* No Failure of Nerve." *College English,* XVIII (November, 1956), 101-102.

Wadsworth, Frank W. "Orwell as a Novelist: The Early Work." *University of Kansas City Review,* XXII (Winter, 1955), 93-99.

————. "Orwell as a Novelist: The Middle Period." *University of Kansas City Review,* XXII (Spring, 1956), 189-194.

————. "Orwell as a Novelist: Orwell's Later Work." *University of Kansas City Review,* XXII (Summer, 1956), 285-290.

West, Anthony. "George Orwell." *Principles and Persuasions.* New York: Harcourt, Brace, 1957, 164-176.

Wilson, Edmund. "Grade-A Essays: Orwell, Sartre, and Highet." *The New Yorker,* XXVI (January 13, 1951), 76 ff.

INDEX

This book was set in Linotype Baskerville, a face known as a transitional design bridging the gap between "old style" and "modern style" faces. The text was printed on 60 lb. Warren's Old Style Antique stock and the covers on Beckett India Antique stock. The book was printed by C. E. Pauley and Co., Inc., Indianapolis, Ind. The cover was printed by offset lithography by Krieger-Ragsdale and Co., Inc. The cover design is by Moroni St. John.